Britain's fastest growing ~~driving~~ school just moved up a ~~gear~~

Top *10* Tips

for selecting a driving school

1. Check that your instructor has a green licence in the windscreen of the car – this indicates that they are fully qualified on the Driving Standards Agency instructor register Part 3 (a pink licence indicates a trainee instructor).

2. Check that the instructor's car has dual controls and is in good condition. Also make sure a spare car is available in case of breakdown.

3. When checking prices, don't assume cheapest is the best. Check out all the added value benefits, discounts for pre-payment, membership of a motoring organisation and post-test tuition (motorway). Check out how long a 'lesson' is. Some driving schools conduct lessons at less than 1 hour each.

4. Check that your driving school can help with the written theory test. You'll have to pass this before you can take your practical test.

5. Make sure your instructor monitors your progress on the official syllabus.

6. Only buy a theory test book that contains the official questions and answers.

7. Apply for your theory test as soon as you start your tuition.

8. Ask your instructor when to apply for your practical test (remember you'll need to pass your theory test first).

9. Get ready for your test by taking regular lessons with a quality instructor (at least an hour, but preferably two per week). Your instructor will advise you on how much tuition you should need.

10. Go for it!

AA Driving Test
Pass
First Time

The **Complete** Guide for Learner Drivers

Jane Gregory BA (Hons), PGCE

AA Publishing

Written by: **Jane Gregory**

Consultants: **Ian Dowd**, ADI
                M D Ellison, ADI
                Janet Goodman, ADI
                Michael Hazell, ADI, Cert Ed, Dip MA
                Sue Hubbard, ADI, Business Development Manager,
                AA The Driving School
The author would also like to thank John Stubbs, AA Head of Technical Policy,
for advice.

Copy editor: **Pam Stagg**

Artwork: **Chris Orr & Associates**

Produced by: **AA Publishing**

© Automobile Association Developments Limited 2000
Reprinted with amendments 2001
Reprinted Feb 2002, March 2004

Traffic signs © Crown copyright. Reproduced with the permission of the Controller
of Her Majesty's Stationery Office.

Published by AA Publishing, a trading name of Automobile Association Developments
Limited, whose registered office is Millstream, Maidenhead Road, Windsor SL4 5GD;
registered number 1878835.

A CIP catalogue record for this book is available from the British Library.

ISBN 0 7495 2446 4 paperback
ISBN 0 7495 2588 6 hardback

A02107

Repro by Anton Graphics, Andover

Printing by Mladinska Knija Tiskarna, Slovenia

Find out more about the AA on www.theAA.com

Contents

Introduction

For most people, passing their driving test is an important step. It's one of the ways in which young people can show that they are growing up and becoming more responsible; like passing exams at school or college, it's an achievement to be proud of, and your pass certificate opens the gate to a whole range of new opportunities.

In this book you'll find help and advice on all the aspects of learning to drive that are covered in your practical and theory tests: the car's controls, the set exercises, legal documents, rules of the road, attitude and hazard awareness, and much more. There are other books available that give advice on particular aspects of learning to drive

– for example, the AA publishes a book of the official questions for the theory test (which you must pass before applying for your practical test), and a question-and-answer guide to the practical test.

This book also tells you how to apply for your theory and practical tests; what to do if you're not successful first time round; and what to look for when buying your first car. Not just for young learner drivers, it will be useful for those learning to drive later in life, or for anyone who has failed their test and wants to improve their skills ready for the next time.

It's important to know that the information you're reading is up-to-date and correct, and who better to check the facts than a panel of top driving instructors? A team from the AA's own Driving School have contributed their knowledge and expertise to ensure accuracy in this book.

As a learner driver, your priorities are to acquire the skills needed for safe and competent driving through taking a course of lessons with an approved driving instructor, and to gain a thorough knowledge of *The Highway Code*. **Pass First Time** is intended to reinforce and complement that learning, and provide a resource for reference between lessons and when preparing for your tests.

We hope you will enjoy reading it, and find it a useful aid to learning to drive.

You and your vehicle

Get into the car...

Remember the order of the pedals from right to left by using 'ABC'– ACCELERATOR, BRAKE, CLUTCH.

So – you're getting ready to go for your first driving lesson! It might help you to feel more confident if you know what to expect when you GET INTO THE CAR.

THE CONTROLS

Look around and find:
- the accelerator pedal
- the brake pedal
- the clutch pedal
- the handbrake (sometimes forgotten but very important!)
- the gear lever

- the steering wheel
- the indicators.

Check that the door is closed, then adjust your seat by moving the base backwards or forwards so that you can comfortably put your hands on the steering wheel at 'ten to two' (or 'quarter to three'), and so that you can fully depress the clutch pedal easily with your left foot. There must be at least 25cm between your chest and the centre boss of the steering wheel. The seat back should be

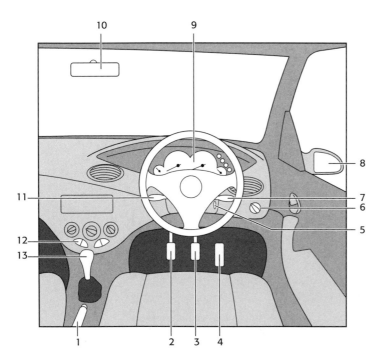

FINDING THE CONTROLS

1 handbrake
2 clutch pedal
3 brake pedal
4 accelerator pedal
5 ignition switch/steering lock
6 lighting switch
7 windscreen wiper and washer
8 side mirror
9 instuments and warning lights
10 rear view mirror
11 direction indicators and horn
12 fog lights
13 gear change lever

upright in a comfortable position. Adjust your head restraint so that its top is at least as high as your eye-level. Fit your seatbelt, making sure the lap strap is well down over the hips and the shoulder strap clear of your neck.

Then press the pedals down, making sure you can press hard on the brake without fully straightening your right leg. In the normal 'manual gearbox' car the clutch pedal will be on the left, then the brake, and the accelerator on the right. Using your left hand, go through the various gear positions. The gears control the speed of the engine relative to the car's speed. First gear is the one you select to start moving, then you change up into second, followed by third, and finally fourth gear. Many cars also have a fifth gear, which is for use on long stretches of driving at fairly high speeds.

In nearly all cars the position you select for the four or five forward gears will be the same (see the diagram), but the position for reverse varies with different models of car – you may need to lift the lever across a 'gate', or press down and then across.

If you are going to drive an **automatic** car, the gear selector looks very different (see diagram below), there are only two pedals (accelerator and brake) and you control the car in a different way (see page 20).

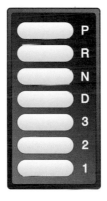

THE INSTRUMENT PANEL

The arrangement of the dashboard will vary slightly from car to car, but there are several items that will appear somewhere on all of them.

Speedometer

Marked in miles/kilometres per hour – measures how fast you're going.

Look in the manufacturer's instruction manual for information about the instrument panel in your own car. It will tell you what to do when any of the lights comes on; in some cases you should stop immediately and get help from a garage – for example, if the oil light comes on. (Driving with it on can seriously damage your engine!)

The head restraints are there to reduce the risk of neck injuries in an accident, so make sure they are correctly adjusted.

Did you know that it's illegal to drive if your windscreen washer system isn't working?

Mileometer

Now often called the odometer, this measures how far the car has been driven. There may also be a trip meter, which measures the distance driven on a particular journey (useful for keeping a check on fuel consumption).

Warning (indicator) lights

For example:

- oil pressure in the engine
- brake system
- fuel level
- battery/alternator
- fasten seat belt reminder
- air bag.

Depending on the age and make of the car, other displays may be located on the panel, such as a clock. You might find the controls for the **lights** there too, but often they are located on the lever that operates the indicators.

There will be a blue light to indicate when your **main beam** headlights are on – normally you use main beam only on roads with no street lights, and you should revert to **dipped headlights** whenever another car approaches, or when you are driving behind another car, to avoid dazzling the driver. **Fog lights** have their own

indicator light on the panel too; again, there are definite times for using these (see page 105).

Take a few minutes to work out where all these indicator lights are – it's important to know, especially when you're driving at night.

A GOOD VIEW ALL ROUND

You also need to adjust the rear view mirror and the door mirrors to give you a good view. *Your use of the mirrors will play a key part in passing your driving test!* So make sure you can see properly in them. (See MSM, page 18.)

Check, too, that you can see out of the car properly when driving (see adjusting your seat, page 12).

Adjust the head restraints so that they don't get in the way of your view of the traffic and of the road behind you, but are at the correct height to protect your head in the event of an accident.

SAFETY FIRST

When you GET INTO THE CAR 'for real' after you've passed your test, or when you're putting in practice between lessons with a qualified driver, there are some other things you should get into the habit

of checking. Your car manual will
have a useful list, but here are some
general safety checks common to all
cars:

- oil and coolant
- windscreen washer liquid
- tyre pressures and condition of
  tyres
- whether you need to fill up with
  fuel (see page 42)
- all windows are free of ice, dirt
  and grease
- all lights and indicators working
- horn in full working order.

Many of these checks aren't just
for your safety, they are *legally*
necessary too.

HOW TO CARRY OUT THE CHECKS

Checking the oil

Do this when the car has been
standing for several hours, and
before you start the engine. Make
sure the car is parked **on a level road
surface** (if you're on a slope the
reading won't be accurate). Pull out
the dipstick and wipe with a cloth;
put it back in as far as it will go, then
pull it out again – the oil should
come about half-way between the
markers. (Some have 'Add oil'
marked on the stick.) Add some

engine oil if it's low, pouring it
through the filler cap. (If you run
out of oil, the engine will seize up
completely.) Some high-performance
engines may require a non-standard
oil – check you car's manual if
you're not sure.

The engine cooling system

The liquid in the radiator is correctly
referred to as 'coolant'. The scenes in
days gone by of radiators boiling on
hill climbs and motorists refilling
them by sometimes unconventional
methods aren't usually seen now, as
the cooling systems in today's cars
tend to be more efficient. Check your
car's handbook for the correct
mixture to add. If appropriate, and
you need to top up the level, unscrew
the coolant cap and top it up
steadily. *Don't do this when the
engine's hot* – you could damage both
yourself and the engine.

Note: you also need to add antifreeze
(see page 36).

Windscreen washer liquid

You can usually see by looking at
the bottle if this needs topping up.
It's best to use a proper windscreen
cleaner, not just washing-up liquid
which can smear the screen (see

Don't let the oil level come higher than the upper marker on the dipstick – this could cause fouling of the spark plugs, and other problems.

The legal tread depth for cars is at least 1.6mm all round the tyre, across the central three-quarters of tyre width; for motorcycles, large vehicles and those that carry passengers it's 1mm.

also page 38). Some screen cleaners will have an additive to help prevent the liquid from freezing on the windscreen in cold weather.

Tyre pressures

Look at your manual to find the correct pressures for the tyres. You can go to a garage or petrol station and use their equipment to check the pressures (often this is free), or you can buy your own tyre pressure gauge. Add air if necessary to bring the tyres to the correct readings. Tyre pressures should be checked when the tyres are **cold** to ensure an accurate reading.

Check tyres for signs of wear and tear and look at the tread pattern. If the wear is uneven it could mean your wheels aren't aligned properly.

Fuel

The fuel gauge will tell you if you're running low. In most cars, you get a bit of warning before you run out completely, but it's better not to risk it, especially if you're driving alone. There's also a risk of getting sediment in the engine if you run the fuel right down.

(See 'All about Fuel', page 40, for what fuel to choose and how to add it – you must be aware of what fuel your vehicle uses, as mistakes can be expensive!)

Front and rear screens

A few minutes cleaning these inside and out before your journey is time well spent, especially if you're about to drive in winter or at night. Low sun can produce glare through a greasy screen, and areas left by faulty wiper blades are a hazard in the dark. Use a clean, damp wash-leather to clean the windows.

Checking the lights

You'll need someone to stand outside the car and help you check that brake lights and indicators are working. If you park close to a reflective surface (such as a garage door), you may be able to see for yourself if something isn't working. Sometimes you'll have to replace a bulb.

All the above need checking before setting out on a long journey; and it's good to get into the habit of **weekly checks**. Check the state of the tyres *every day*.

If you're parked in front of another car, or at a garage, it's often possible to look in the mirror while depressing the brake pedal, and check the lights are working in the reflection.

TEST YOUR UNDERSTANDING
OF THIS SECTION

1. What does ABC stand for?

2. What should you do if the oil light comes on and stays lit?

3. What should you check regularly on your car?

4. How do you check the oil?

5. What is the required legal depth of tread for car tyres?

Answers on page 178

Can you handle it?

Older cars often need the choke pulled out part or all of the way to get started, then you push the choke in once you're underway. However, most modern cars benefit from electronic fuel injection.

The letters MSM stand for Mirror, Signal, Manoeuvre – it's well worth memorising this right away.

Right then – off we go.

You'll have chosen your qualified instructor (for advice on this see 'Choosing an instructor', page 29), and you're bracing yourself to make the car move along the road for the first time – hopefully in the direction you intend.

We'll assume you're learning in an ordinary manual car. (For the starting sequence in an automatic, see page 20) Are you sitting comfortably? Can you see clearly all around? Is your seat belt fastened?

Always start the car with the gears at 'neutral'.

The handbrake should be *on*.

Wait for your instructor's signal then turn the key to *start the car!*

USING THE GEARS

Depress the clutch pedal, select first gear, and check your mirror to see if it is safe to move off. Don't forget to look over your shoulder.

Your instructor will show you how to use the clutch and the accelerator smoothly together to move off steadily.

Use your indicator if necessary before pulling out.

Then check again over your shoulder, release the handbrake and *move off*.

Move up through the gears smoothly, and down again as you approach road junctions, roundabouts or bends.

When you take your driving test, you'll need to show that you can control the car smoothly and safely. Obviously, don't pull out into the path of other motorists; and try to avoid stalling the car!

If you *do* stall – don't panic, but put the handbrake on and the gears in neutral and start the whole sequence again.

GETTING THE HABIT

Get into *good habits* from the start; put both hands on the wheel and keep them there unless you're changing gear or using the handbrake. It may look cool to cruise along with one arm resting on the window ledge, but it certainly isn't safe!

Don't drive along with your hand resting on the gear lever either.

New drivers often think they can never go as slowly as, say, a cyclist in front of them; it's good practice sometimes to see *just how slowly* you can manoeuvre – which takes us on to reversing, a routine which should *always* be done *slowly and carefully!*

REVERSING

It's important to feel just as confident about reversing as you do about normal driving. The Driving Test requires you to carry out a reversing manoeuvre such as:

- reversing into a parking bay at the test centre
- reversing to park between two cars, parallel with the kerb
- reversing round a corner
- turning in the road (see right).

The key to successful reversing is good observation of the traffic and road conditions around you, and good use of your mirrors and of the car's controls. You should also use the rear window.

There are several places where it's not safe to reverse, for example into a busy main road, or near a children's play area. Often you can make the procedure safer by driving on a little further before you start, or even driving round the block.

For more advice on reversing, see *The Highway Code.*

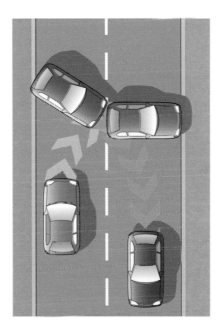

The reason you need to check over your shoulder as well as using the mirror is that there will be a *blind spot* just over your right shoulder, that isn't visible in the mirror.

Did you know that you are allowed to have your seat belt unfastened while reversing? It's the only time you can do so while driving.

If you haven't got your foot on the brake when you go into Drive, the car may start moving on its own – disconcerting, and possibly dangerous, especially if you're parked behind another car!

DRIVING AN AUTOMATIC CAR

When you drive in other countries – for example, Australia or the USA – you'll find that a great many of the cars on the road are **automatics**. This means they select the appropriate gear for your speed for you as you drive.

The good news is that if you're a competent driver of a 'manual' car, you'll have very little trouble in getting used to driving an automatic. Similarly, if you go back to a manual car after driving an automatic, you'll be able to adjust without any problems.

If you take your test in an automatic you are *not qualified* to drive a manual car. So it probably makes sense, if you can, to take your test in a manual, then you're covered for any car you may later drive.

We've already looked at how the appearance and controls of an automatic car differ from a manual (see page 13), now we'll deal with start-up procedure and general driving.

Starting an automatic car

The car won't start unless the gear lever is in **Park** or **Neutral**, so check.

Then start the engine and *put your foot on the brake.*

Select **Drive** from the gears, release the handbrake and slowly lift your foot off the brake; move it to the accelerator as the car picks up speed. Use the accelerator and brake pedals with your right foot *only.*

As you pick up speed the automatic transmission will change the gears up, or change them down when you brake. Automatics are great on hills or in a line of traffic because you don't have to hold the car on the brakes and clutch. However, they do have some disadvantages; one is that they tend to use more petrol than similarly-sized manual cars.

FOUR-WHEEL DRIVE VEHICLES

Slightly different skills are needed to drive these; the manufacturer's instructions will explain how and when to select the four-wheel drive option.

TEST YOUR UNDERSTANDING OF THIS SECTION

1. What should you check before starting the engine?

2. What do the letters MSM stand for, and what do they mean for you as a driver?

3. Why do you need to check over your shoulder as well as looking in the mirror?

4. Does reversing into a parking bay form part of the driving test?

5. How do you move off when driving an automatic car?

Answers on page 179

Are you legal?

People with disabilities can apply for a licence when they're 16.

DOCUMENTS

Before you can get into a car and drive it on a public road you need to have the right pieces of paper to prove you're legally allowed to drive.

Provisional licence

You can get an application form for a provisional licence from any Post Office, up to two months before your 17th birthday. Ask for Form D1. The licence consists of a photocard and a paper counterpart. You can also get forms by phoning the **Driver and Vehicle Licensing Agency** (DVLA) on 01792 772151.

Form D750 has a space for your photograph and signature.

Take care when providing your signature – it has to be right, because it will be scanned on to both the photo licence and the paper counterpart.

You'll get a leaflet with advice about the right sort of photo to send:
- no shadow
- not too light or dark
- no headgear
- no curtain background.

If you can, send a current UK passport as your identity document. If you don't have one, you can send your birth or adoption certificate (not a photocopy), but you'll need to get your photograph certified by a person with official status (suitable people are listed on the application form).

Insurance certificate

You can't drive without a valid insurance certificate that covers you for a minimum of third party liability (see 'Insurance', page 25). If you're learning with a recognised driving school, you'll be covered by their insurance while in the driving school car; but in your own car, you need to make sure you're properly covered.

Vehicle Registration Document

This document records the make and model of the vehicle, and gives details of the registered keeper. You have to notify the DVLA in Swansea when you buy or sell a car, or if you change your name or address.

Note: as a record of the vehicle's history this is sometimes refered to as the 'log book' – however, see page 24.

Tax disc

This is the name most people use for the vehicle Excise Duty disc; every car has to have an up-to-date tax disc displayed on the windscreen. You replace it with a new disc every six or 12 months. (The cost will vary, depending on the size of your car's engine and emissions.)

MOT certificate

Cars and motor cycles have to be MOT'd three years after they're first registered, and then every year. The aim of the MOT is to check that your vehicle is mechanically safe to drive, but also that it's environmentally sound (i.e. it docs not exceed the permitted levels of toxic emissions).

It is illegal to drive without an MOT certificate if your vehicle should have one – unless you're on your way to a pre-arranged appointment for an MOT.

You have to produce some or all of the following documents when asked by a police officer:
- **driving licence**
- **insurance certificate**
- **MOT certificate.**

If you can't produce them on the spot, you have to take them to a police station within seven days.

Your supervisor

You can't go it alone when you're learning to drive; when you're practising between lessons, without your instructor, you have to be *supervised*.

The person with you has to be over 21 and be the holder of a full driving licence – and they must have had their licence for three years or more.

Log book

This is a new booklet from the **Driving Standards Agency** to help learner drivers. It's not a legal document, but it may become so in the future, and it could help you pass your test.

Your instructor can use it to write down everything you learn in your driving lessons and to keep a record of your progress – and there's a quick-reference list of the topics in the Theory Test (see page 154).

INSURANCE – LEVELS OF COVER

Third Party insurance

This is usually available as **'Third Party, Fire and Theft'** cover. It's a basic insurance policy that covers you for damage to another person's car and allows you to claim on the other driver's insurance if you are involved in an accident that wasn't your fault.

Note: 'third party' means a person, or property, outside the vehicle; the 'first party' is the driver and the 'second party' the passenger.

Comprehensive insurance

This kind of policy covers damage to your vehicle even when the accident was your fault.

There are all sorts of 'catches' that apply to insurance policies, however, so –

read the small print!

You might find that some of the following apply:

- **Excess** – This means that the insurance company won't pay, for example, the first £50 or £100 of your claim and you have to pay it yourself.

- **'Named drivers'** – The insurance may only cover specific people named in the policy. You pay more if more people are covered to drive the car; it's most expensive if the car's covered for anyone to drive.

- **'Knock-for-knock'** – different insurance companies have different rules about whose policy actually pays out in the event of an accident where there has been damage to vehicles.

- **'No-claims' bonus** – in some cases people will choose not to claim, but settle the matter between themselves, so that their no-claims bonus won't be affected.

If you are involved in an accident with someone who isn't insured, or if you can't trace the person responsible, the Motor Insurers' Bureau has a fund for this purpose.

What about driving someone else's car?

Again, the best thing is to check the wording of the policy carefully to see whether you are covered to drive the other person's car.

L-PLATES

While you're learning, you must have red L-plates at the front and back of your car. They must be displayed vertically, and not placed in the window obscuring your view.

(*Note:* in Wales you display either red D-plates, red L-plates, or both.)

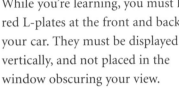

There is a legal requirement for L-plates to be 178mm square, with the 'L' 40 x 102 x 38mm.

OWNERSHIP DOCUMENTS AND SECOND-HAND CARS

When you buy or sell a car, certain documents have to change hands.

See page 23 for the **Vehicle Registration Document** or 'V5'. This form has different sections – one part is for you to send to the DVLA on change of ownership, and another part goes to the new owner for use as a temporary registration document.

If you buy a brand new car, the dealer will usually have registered it, but if you buy a second-hand car in a private sale, it's up to you to re-register the car in your name.

You'll also need to contact your insurer about adjusting your cover, which may mean cancelling your old policy and taking out a new one.

EYESIGHT

It doesn't matter at all if you want to learn to drive and you wear glasses or contact lenses. All that matters is that you can see clearly with them.

BUT –

- you must *wear* your glasses or contact lenses whenever you drive – and of course, wear them during your driving test.

The eyesight test

Your driving test begins with an eyesight test. You have to be able to read a normal number plate at a minimum distance of 20.5 metres (about 67½ feet).

Most people don't have another eye test to see if they are safe to drive until they apply for an extension of their licence at the age of 70, and random tests suggest that as many as 4 million of the 33 million drivers on the road actually can't see well enough to drive. So it's important to include regular eye tests in your ongoing attempts to be a safe driver once you've passed your test (see Part 4, 'Taking the test – and beyond').

If you've had laser surgery to improve your eyesight, you should declare this when you apply for your provisional licence. You should also inform the DVLA if you suffer from glaucoma.

TEST YOUR UNDERSTANDING
OF THIS SECTION

1. What document must you have before you start driving?

2. What information is recorded in a log book?

3. What qualifications must a person have to supervise a learner driver?

4. What is an 'excess' on a car insurance policy?

5. At what point in your driving test will you be given an eyesight test, and what does the eyesight test consist of?

Answers on page 180

Who's in charge?

You can expect to pay up to £20* for each driving lesson, so you're going to expect good value for your hard-earned cash – or, for some fortunate people, their parents' hard-earned cash!

How do you go about deciding who will teach you to drive?

You want to be sure that your driving instructor is fully qualified to teach you all the skills you need to pass your driving test.

CHOOSING AN INSTRUCTOR

It's interesting that in some other countries (Germany, for example), a driving lesson costs a lot more than in the UK – around £50 – and the job of being a driving instructor is seen as a profession.

Perhaps we don't always give our qualified driving instructors the respect they should receive; so, make sure you choose an instructor who is a professional, and then do your bit

You can feel confident you've made the right choice if you decide to learn with the AA's Driving School. *All* its staff are fully qualified driving instructors.

*Correct at time of publication

by treating them as such – it should make for a positive learner/teacher relationship!

Ask around

It's a good idea to find out from your friends whether they've been impressed by a particular instructor, and which are good reliable driving schools.

That was then – this is now!

Remember, you need *up-to-date* information – so, talk to someone who has learned to drive *recently!*

What does 'fully qualified' mean?

Your instructor should display an **ADI certificate** on the windscreen of their car. This shows that they have passed the Driving Standards Authority's tests to become an Approved Driving Instructor (ADI).

Note: an ADI certificate is green – an instructor who displays a pink certificate is a trainee.

Buyer beware!

Price is an important factor when choosing your driving instructor, so find out whether you can benefit from any special deals, such as a discount when you book a block of lessons in advance.

For example, the AA's Driving School offers a block of 12 lessons for a discount of £24*.

If you find a lesson price that's surprisingly low, before you decide on it, ask yourself

'WHY?'

Is there some reason why the cost is so cheap?

And don't forget to ask about the car you'll be learning in, too.

Is it modern and reliable?
Is it insured?

Anyone who accepts payment for giving driving lessons has to be an Approved Driving Instructor, or at least a trainee licence-holder.

*Correct at time of publication

HOW MANY LESSONS DO I NEED?

Of course this varies from person to person, but it may be useful to know that many people need more than 30 hours of lessons.

Each lesson usually last two hours. Some driving schools offer a concentrated intensive course, but most instructors recommend learning over a period of a few months or more, backed up by practice with a supervisor.

Your driving instructor will help with information about when you are ready to take the test, and when to apply for your Theory and Practical tests.

Don't forget the supervisor

In addition to the ADI who will provide your formal lessons, you need a suitable person to supervise you when you're practising between lessons (see page 24).

DON'T FORGET THE THEORY TEST!

It's part of the instructor's job to help you prepare for your **Theory Test** as well as the practical driving test.

It's definitely a good idea to prepare for the Theory Test *at the same time* as you're having driving lessons. The two tests, Practical and Theory, have many things in common – it's all about making you a safer driver.

A good driving school should provide practice Theory Test questions that you can work through before you take the Theory Test for real.

For more on the Theory Test, see page 154.

Statistics show that if you prepare for both tests at the same time, you improve your chances of passing them both first time.

TEST YOUR UNDERSTANDING OF THIS SECTION

1. What should you bear in mind when choosing a driving instructor?

2. What is an ADI certificate?

3. What does the law say about insurance and learner drivers?

4. Can you pay a friend to teach you to drive?

5. Why should you prepare for your practical and theory tests at the same time?

Answers on page 181

Look after your car...

AND IT WILL HELP LOOK AFTER YOU!

If you want to be a good, safe driver, it makes sense to *look after your car*.

You'll know that if your car is unreliable and lets you down, you're likely to become angry and frustrated trying to fix it when you're late getting to somewhere important, or for picking up children from school etc. So when you've got the car going again, your driving will be more erratic, your concentration won't be so good and you're more likely to have an accident.

Every driver should be able to cope with standard maintenance jobs.

Listed on the next pages are some parts of the car that will need to be checked to make sure they are in good working order.

If you're driving your own car in a country where they drive on the right, you can buy headlight converters to change the angle of the beam. But don't forget to remove them when you return to the UK.

The hazard warning system should work whether or not you have the engine switched on.

LIGHTS

All the lights should work, and none of them should be missing.

Check you have:
- two **main beam** headlamps
- two **dipped beam** headlamps

and that for each pair, the two lamps match each other in size and shape, and give out light of a similar intensity.

(See 'I'm right behind you!', in Part 3. Some motorists have fitted lights which are too glaring, and use them to intimidate others.)

Check that the lights are angled correctly – main beam: roughly horizontal, dipped beam: angled towards the kerb (left).

Give the headlights a good clean (soapy water and a soft cloth is fine), as dirt can quickly build up and reduce their effectiveness.

Rear lamps

All cars must have two red lights at the back as well as the white lights at the front; again, they need cleaning, and a check to see whether the bulbs are working.

Brake lights

All cars built since 1 January 1971 must have at least **two red brake lights**.

Cars built since 1 April 1980 must also have **one rear fog lamp** (many have two). (See 'It's different at night', page 100 for when to use fog lamps, and when not to.)

Reflectors

Your car must have two red reflectors fitted to the back – one on each side.

Indicators

Most modern cars have flashing amber lights as indicators; check these work properly.

However, it's still legal for old cars to have older types of indicators.

Hazard Warning Lights

Check that when you turn on the car's hazard warning switch, all the indicator lights flash in time with each other. (See page 119 for when to use these.)

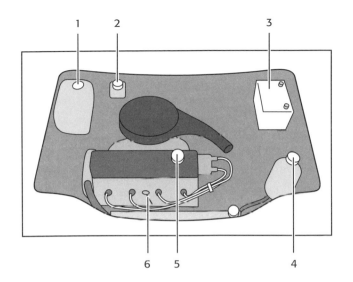

UNDER THE BONNET

1 windscreen washer reservoir
2 brake fluid reservoir
3 battery
4 cooling system reservoir
5 engine oil filler cap
6 engine oil dipstick

Try to use the same type of oil each time; your car manual will have a chart that tells you which oil is best for your particular model.

Dispose of used oil properly (*not* down the drain) – protect the environment!

OIL

Modern cars don't get through as much oil as some older ones, but all cars use up a certain amount.

Check your engine oil every 500km (300 miles) or before starting out on a long journey. (See 'Checking the oil', page 15.)

Changing the oil

This usually forms part of the car's regular service and will be done for you at the garage – it is a good idea to let them do it, as there are legal requirements about disposing of used oil.

Allow the engine to cool down before you open the cap! And open the cap *slowly* to allow the pressure to reduce slowly.

COOLANT AND ANTIFREEZE

The cooling system contains a glycol-based coolant, which protects against the effects of high and low temperatures, and also against corrosion.

While the engine's running the system is under pressure, so the temperature may sometimes rise to over 100°C – for example, if you have to wait in traffic for a while on a hot day. In modern cars this shouldn't be a problem, but you'll need to check the coolant level later and if necessary add a little *clean* water.

Freeze protection

The coolant is designed to stay in the system all year and should be able to handle temperatures down to -30°C.

However, if the coolant isn't concentrated enough, you may need to add antifreeze. Remember what we said earlier about 'That was then – this is now!' Well-intentioned advice from older motorists about adding antifreeze may not be relevant for your car. Ask your garage to check the coolant concentration, and also to recommend a good-quality antifreeze.

THE BATTERY

Again, many modern cars are supplied with the kind of sealed battery that requires no maintenance. If your car *does* have a battery that needs topping up, then you'll sometimes need to add de-ionised water to it.

Depending on the make and type of car, there are several more fluids to keep a check on:

These include:
- brake fluid
- special oil for the transmission in automatic cars (also used for cars with power-assisted steering)
- screen wash fluid
- headlamp washer fluid.

BRAKE FLUID

Take care if you have any dealings with this – it's poisonous. If it comes into contact with your car's paintwork it will damage it.

You can check the level of fluid in the container; look for 'MIN' and 'MAX' markers to indicate the correct level. If it's below the mark, check with your garage, because you need to find out and deal with the cause of the problem. (Many cars now include an indicator light to alert you to low levels.)

Your car manual will tell you how often the brake fluid should be changed.

Always use **new** brake fluid – old fluid is liable to deteriorate.

AUTOMATIC TRANSMISSION FLUID

It's vital that this is kept at the correct level in order for the automatic transmission to work effectively.

The oil level will be checked when the car is serviced by your garage. If you are not sure about this for any reason, then get it checked specially.

Wear protective gloves when handling *any* of these fluids.

Cars with power-assisted steering are easier to manoeuvre because the mechanism does some of the hard work for you. Power-assisted steering is increasingly becoming a standard feature.

Don't try to clear your screen while facing into direct sunlight – the screen will fog up.

SCREEN WASH FLUID

The container for this is usually located towards one side of the engine. It's simply a case of unscrewing the cap and adding clean water, perhaps containing some screen-wash liquid.

You'll need to do this quite frequently during bad weather – and it's a legal requirement to keep it topped up (see page 15). While you're driving behind any large vehicle in rain, or when there's mud on the road, spray from the vehicle in front can coat your screen with particles, and if there's a low sun in front as well you will very quickly find you can't see anything unless you can clear your screen.

You can get similar problems in fine summer weather but this time it's caused by small insects (bugs) sticking to the windscreen!

In freezing weather the screen-wash mechanism won't work and you run the risk of water freezing on the windscreen; clean ice off all glass surfaces *before* you start driving (see 'Stormy weather', page 102) and use a proper winter-grade additive in the screen wash.

HEADLAMP WASHER FLUID

Some cars are fitted with a headlamp washer system. Again, look for the filler cap in the engine compartment.

WINDSCREEN WIPERS

You need to keep the wipers in good working order. A damaged wiper blade will fail to clear the screen properly, and leave smears or arcs of dirt, making it dangerous to drive because your field of vision is reduced.

You can clean the blades with a soft cloth, but you may need to replace them if they've become hardened or cracked – maybe as a result of being frozen to the screen, or being exposed to heat, salt or the wrong sort of cleaning agent.

How to change the blades

- Turn off the ignition when the wipers are in the upright position.
- Lift up the wiper arm slightly.
- Use the release mechanism to remove the damaged blade.
- Replace with a new one.

SEAT BELTS

Make sure that these are in good working order, then keep an eye on them for signs of wear, non-functioning mechanisms etc.

The seat belts will be checked as part of the MOT.

The laws about different types of seat belts aren't straightforward, but as a guide:

- cars built after 1 January 1965 must have front seat belts
- cars built after 31 March 1981 require lap belts as well
- cars built after 31 March 1987 require rear seat belts.

See 'It's your responsibility' (page 142) for what you need to know about passengers and seat belt law.

Types of seat belt

Unless you've got a fairly old car, your seat belts will be of the **inertia reel** kind which extend to fit the passenger. The older **static** belts have to be adjusted manually. (See also 'It's your responsibility', pages 142–4.)

Avoid getting seat belts twisted, as this can add to injuries in an accident. Always replace seat belts after an accident.

Where there are seat belts fitted they *must* be worn, except in the case of people holding an exemption certificate for medical reasons.

ALL ABOUT FUEL

The main things to be aware of here are:

- taking care you don't run out
- using the right kind
- knowing how to operate a petrol pump.

How much fuel in the tank?

Remember to check the fuel gauge before you set out (see page 16 for a reminder of why this is important).

If your fuel gauge doesn't work –

GET IT SEEN TO!

It's not a good idea (because of fire risk) to carry a full can of fuel in the car in case of emergency; but you *could* sensibly carry an empty can, so that you could walk to a garage.

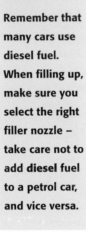

Remember that many cars use diesel fuel. When filling up, make sure you select the right filler nozzle – take care not to add diesel fuel to a petrol car, and vice versa.

Which type of fuel?

By now you'll be well aware of the government drive for all cars to use unleaded fuel.

Leaded petrol has been replaced by **LRP** (Lead Replacement Petrol); you might still see '4-star' on the pump.

On modern petrol cars the fuel tank filler neck is designed to be too narrow too allow you to put in LRP fuel; see 'Putting fuel in the car' on page 42.

CATALYTIC CONVERTERS

If you have a petrol-fuelled car built after 1992, it will be fitted with a catalytic converter. *Catalyst* means something that enables a chemical change to take place; the catalytic converter, which is located in the car's exhaust system, converts pollutant gases into less harmful gases.

Owning a car fitted with a *catalytic converter* **should encourage you to drive even more carefully**. This is because they are fairly easily damaged – for example, if you were to back the car into a wall and hit the exhaust pipe, if unburnt fuel enters the converter, or if you drive through deep water or deep snow.

Unburnt fuel can enter the converter if you:

- repeatedly turn the starter key because the engine is cold, thus 'flooding the engine'
- 'bump-start' the car, by pushing or towing.

Try to avoid these situations by:

- making sure as many electrical components as possible are turned off when you're starting up: e.g., lights, radio, front and rear window heaters, fans. Once the engine is running you can switch on those you need.
- instead of bump-starting, use **jump-leads** to start the car by linking up to another car battery.

PUTTING FUEL IN THE CAR

It can be quite alarming to find, once you're the proud possessor of a 'pass' certificate, that you haven't a clue how to put fuel in your car!

So, here's a useful list of reminders for YOUR FIRST TRIP TO THE GARAGE!

- Have you got cash, or a credit or debit card, to pay for the fuel? It's all too easy to fill the car up and then find you've forgotten your wallet!
- Which side of the car is your filler cap? Once you've sorted this out, then you'll know which side of the pump to park at the garage.
- How does your car's filler cap open? It helps to know this *before* you arrive at the garage. On older makes of car the cap could be unscrewed manually, but on most modern cars it unlocks with a key, and sometimes even with a release lever inside the car.
- As soon as you have parked in the correct position at the garage, *switch off your engine* – this is very important, as fuel is highly combustible.
- For the same reason – ***don't smoke!***
- You'll see a row of pumps with the fuel descriptions written on them, and also coloured caps to help

you further. The pump with the **green cap** will be the one for **unleaded fuel**. The **diesel** pump may be **black** or **yellow**. There may be other variations, e.g. 'Super Plus Unleaded'; if you're in any doubt, ask for advice, or check your car manual.

- Remove the filler cap.
- Lift the fuel dispenser from the pump and place it into your tank as far as it will go.
- Check that the display on the pump is at zero.
- Squeeze the trigger and carry on filling until you have as much as you need, or until the pump cuts off automatically. Don't attempt to fill the tank any further after this.
- Replace the fuel dispenser and the filler cap.
- Use a piece of the paper towel roll provided to wipe off any fuel around the fuel inlet (or from your own hands, feet etc!)
- Note the number of the pump you used, and then go and pay, and drive away. Some pumps will accept credit and debit cards.
- *Do not use a mobile phone on the garage forecourt* as this can interfere with the controls of the pumps.

ENVIRONMENTALLY FRIENDLY

You'll know that as well as using unleaded fuel, one way to keep your motoring as 'green' as possible is to aim for maximum *fuel efficiency*.

There are several ways to achieve this:

- Have your car serviced regularly by a reliable garage. Correct *engine tuning* is a must to keep emissions to a minimum.
- Keep your tyres at the right pressures – driving on under-inflated tyres uses up more fuel.
- Avoid harsh acceleration.

- Don't drive too fast – speed increases fuel consumption. But *do* drive in the highest possible gear for the speed you're driving at.
- Don't leave a roof rack on the car when you don't need one; roof racks cause 'drag' and make the car less aerodynamic.
- Try to plan journeys to avoid crawling through traffic for long periods – use city Park and Ride schemes, or even go by bike!

Most garages in the UK are self-service, but when travelling in some other parts of the world you may have your car filled up by an attendant.

The more you can learn about maintenance and the various parts of the car, the more confident you will be about checking that the person who services your car is doing a thorough job.

TEST YOUR UNDERSTANDING OF THIS SECTION

1. When would you need to fit headlight converters?

2. What are the legal requirements concerning the fitting of fog lights?

3. If you're driving on a hot day and the temperature gauge is close to the red zone, do you have to stop driving immediately?

4. What is meant by power-assisted steering?

5. Why is it dangerous to drive when your windscreen washer fluid container is empty?

6. Are passengers travelling in the rear of your car legally required to wear seat belts?

7. What is the purpose of a catalytic converter?

8. What safety precautions should you observe when visiting a garage to fill up with fuel?

9. When you have finished filling up with fuel, is it correct procedure to wait a moment, and then add a bit more?

10. In what ways can you do your best to be a 'green' motorist?

Answers on page 182–3

PART 2

On the road

Motorists with attitude

In 20% of road accidents where there are casualties, at least one of the drivers involved has passed their test recently (within the previous three years).

While you're learning to drive, you'll probably hear a good deal about the virtues of *defensive driving*. This means anticipating hazards, being aware of what other motorists and pedestrians may do, and avoiding taking risks.

Often people who have just passed their test and are raring to go aren't too keen on being told to adopt a cautious approach at all times on the road.

Think about how you would respond to these two statements:

- I aim to be a careful and safety-conscious driver.
- I intend to be a fast and skilful driver.

To many young drivers, the second one sounds a whole lot more appealing than the first. It doesn't help that the word 'courtesy' almost always comes after the word 'old-fashioned'!

Research has shown that young drivers tend not to develop the ability to anticipate hazards successfully until they are older and more experienced (see 'Hazard awareness', page 52). Driving instructors aim to teach some hazard awareness skills, and questions on this form part of the **Theory Test**.

Young male drivers have a higher risk than other groups of being involved in accidents.

WHY ARE YOUNG DRIVERS MORE AT RISK?

Passing your driving test seems to have become something of an initiation ritual in our society, especially for males; it's as if getting through the test is part of becoming an adult. Maybe that's why getting your licence can be followed by an urge to drive too fast and 'show off' to passengers and other drivers.

However –

if you don't want to end up as 'just another statistic', having a positive approach to road safety *is the only way to go.*

A CAR IS NOT AN OFFENSIVE WEAPON

This sounds obvious; but drivers often subconsciously see their car as an extension of themselves, and the way they drive as an expression of their personality.

You only have to think of the hundreds of films that have been made in which reckless car chases are shown as dangerous but glamorous, to realise that a car is rather more than just a means of getting from A to B.

In one-fifth of accidents involving people 19 years old and under, only one car is involved.

Road rage

The AA's Road Safety Unit has carried out extensive research into what makes people engage in road rage. Some of the reasons put forward to explain it are:

- frustration at being kept waiting in traffic congestion
- aggravation if your most cherished possession – your car – has been, or is at risk of being, damaged
- noise: the din of surrounding vehicles, and car radios, can lead to stress and aggression
- hot weather: high temperatures, at times of the year when holiday jams can occur, do seem to make matters worse!

White Van Man

It seems appropriate to devote a special mention to this folk hero of our times.

There are two million vans on the roads in Britain today, and the stereotype of 'White Van Man' as one of the worst offenders for aggressive driving doesn't do their reputation any good at all. However, things are set to improve with the introduction of a 'Good Van Code', similar to the many schemes which truck drivers already take part in to improve *their* reputation as safe drivers.

Did you know that if you collect six or more penalty points within two years of passing your test, you'll lose your licence and have to start again as a learner. (Road Traffic [New Drivers] Act, 1997.)

ATTITUDES TO SPEED

Very often, drivers' attitude problems are about *their attitude to speed limits*.

Problems arise when people drive at a speed which is *inappropriate* for the conditions – type of road, visibility and weather, etc.

It's amazing but some people think:
- that speed limits are only meant for people with poor reaction times
- that 'no overtaking' regulations are only meant for people with less powerful cars.

Attitudes such as these explain why avoidable accidents still happen.

Speed and motorway driving

You may notice that you're tempted to allow other drivers to dictate the speed at which you drive when you're on a motorway. People who observe the speed limits on other roads can suddenly start to behave quite differently once they're on the motorway!

Speed and your passengers

Recent research* shows that the presence of a young male *passenger* will have an effect on the speed of the *driver*. He or she will drive faster than usual. Passengers, on the other hand, generally wish the driver would slow down!

Don't make the same mistake again

It also seems that people don't learn from experience:
- drivers are often involved in the same kind of accident twice.

So – if you're unlucky enough to have an accident, or even a 'near-miss', try to ask yourself *what you can learn* from the experience to help prevent the same type of accident happening next time.

Your attitude to risk-taking in general is likely to be reflected in your attitude to taking risks on the road.

Frank McKenna, Department of Psychology, University of Reading

Your Theory Test is likely to contain a question on *coasting*, or letting the car run downhill in neutral. This leads to loss of control of your braking.

You may also be asked about the *two-second rule*. This means keeping at a distance of a minimum of two seconds behind the vehicle in front. *'Only a fool breaks the two-second rule.'*

WHAT CAUSES ROAD ACCIDENTS TO HAPPEN?

Firstly, it's no good blaming it on the car!

- 95% of accidents are caused by **people** – not by mechanical or other problems.

Some of the most frequent causes of accidents are:

- the driver losing control of the car
- the driver losing concentration
- cars crossing the path of other vehicles
- rear-end shunts.

You're less likely to have an accident if you:

- drive at an appropriate speed, keeping full control of the car
- don't follow so closely behind the car in front that you can't stop if necessary to avoid running into the back of it
- don't overtake and then 'cut in' on other drivers.

We'll look in more detail at driving behaviour (good and bad) in Part 3, 'How am I driving?' (page 114).

TEST YOUR UNDERSTANDING
OF THIS SECTION

1. Who has the fastest reaction time – young motorists or older people?

2. What is the best speed to drive at?

3. Why do people sometimes drive too fast on motorways?

4. Should you 'coast' downhill to save fuel?

5. What is the 'two-second rule', and what does it mean?

Answers on page 184

I didn't even see him...

Remember OAP – Observe, Anticipate, Plan.

As well as the hazards described here, always expect the unexpected!

HAZARD AWARENESS

How often does a motorist protest that the accident happened before they had time to realise the person they hit was there?

A recent research programme*, in which volunteers view videos to test their hazard awareness, has shown that new drivers don't generally perceive as many of the potential hazards as those who have been driving for longer. (But see 'Mobile phones', page 58.)

ANTICIPATION

Some accidents will, of course, inevitably happen, but part of your instructor's job while teaching you to drive is to help you learn to anticipate problems before they happen.

Anticipation involves:

- noticing what's happening around you while you're driving
- anticipating what you might expect to happen next
- deciding what you should do about it.

Anticipation is one of the **key skills** you need to be a safe driver, in addition to:

- observation
- concentration

and

- forward planning.

OBSERVATION

For drivers, *this means more than just looking.*

It should involve *all* your senses; you might *hear* a hedge cutter just around the corner, or *smell* grass being cut.

It means *looking for information.*

*Frank McKenna, Department of Psychology, University of Reading

Train yourself to *scan* as much of the road as you can in your field of vision, to give you more time to decide what action to take if you see a **hazard** coming up.

On the look-out for hazards

Think about the times and places where you're most likely to run into hazards on the road; such as the rush hour, or the end of the school day.

Times to take even more care than usual of course include driving in bad weather or at night; but you're also at risk when you have to *slow down suddenly*, or *make a right or left turn* at a junction where you can't see clearly all around.

Areas to be particularly careful are:

- where there are parked vehicles
- around pedestrian crossings
- at roundabouts and junctions
- near entrances to schools.

Don't forget – you may have to deal with more than one hazard at a time!

Don't forget – MSM!

One in three of road accident fatalities are pedestrians or cyclists.

Parked vehicles

Watch out for:

- a child suddenly running out between parked cars (look and see if there's an ice-cream van on the opposite side of the road)
- a cyclist riding close to the parked cars – you may have to pull out further to overtake them
- car doors opening into the road space
- cars pulling out from the parked lines.

Pedestrian crossings

Get to know the different types of pedestrian crossings; you'll need this information in your driving test. The diagram below shows the road markings leading up to a crossing. (See also page 74.)

When approaching a zebra crossing – *slow down and be prepared to stop.*

At pelican, puffin and toucan crossings –

- *stop* if the lights are red

- *give way to pedestrians* if the amber lights are flashing

- *give way to cyclists* on a toucan crossing.

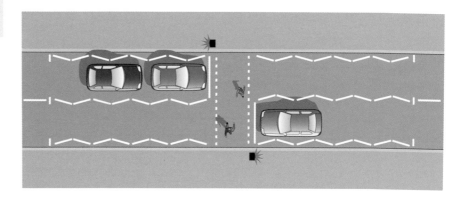

Roundabouts and junctions

Anticipation plays a big part here, as you have to position your car correctly in advance.

Get in the appropriate *lane* (if there are lanes) in good time, and *slow down* enough to be able to make the turn in a safe and controlled manner. (See 'It's in the rules', pages 70–3, for more on lanes and roundabouts.)

Motorcycles

Motorcycles are another possible hazard to be aware of.

Like bicycles, they can be blown off course in high winds, and sometimes they're surprisingly difficult to see.

Also, check your door mirrors on both sides for motorcycles filtering between lanes in queues of traffic.

At some angles, even a lamp post can hide a motorcyclist.

Cyclists and horse riders

You need to exercise caution when behind a cyclist near a junction or roundabout; it's safest not to overtake, but to stay behind them, as they may change lanes unexpectedly.

Cyclists are more at risk than car drivers when there are strong winds, and could be blown off course. So, give them plenty of room.

Keep a good distance between your car and anyone riding a horse; avoid revving the engine as you overtake! Remember, too, to *anticipate* that they might be ahead of you and out of your field of vision on narrow country lanes; slow down, and be prepared to stop.

The reason motorcyclists have their headlamps on in daylight is to make them more visible to other road users.

CONCENTRATION

You can't afford to let your concentration slip even for a moment when you're driving.

At high speeds, the total distance you need to see the hazard, brake and come to a stop can be as much as 96 metres (or 24 car lengths) – that's at 70mph. (See 'Stopping distances', page 84.)

So if you weren't *fully awake*, or if you were *distracted* for some reason, you might fail to stop in time.

You can be distracted by many things, including:
- roadside distractions
- passengers
- pets
- information overload
- mobile phones.

Roadside distractions

These include eye-catching posters; pedestrians who attract your attention for some reason; and (least excusable) turning to look at the scene of an accident as you drive past.

Passengers

Passengers can distract you by sudden movements or incessant talk – all parents have different approaches to controlling their children while in the car, and different views on how much noise they can tolerate on a scale from zero to bedlam. It's important to have children strapped securely into a child seat, or the back seat for older children. (See 'It's your responsibility', page 142.)

Pets

As with children, it's just as important to convey animals properly in the car, so that they don't distract you. A harness designed to be fastened through the seat belt is available for dogs.

Information overload

Compared with someone learning to drive 20 or 30 years ago, you now have so much more to watch all at once.

Road signs, traffic hazards such as motorway lanes merging, or road-works, all compete for your attention and demand constant decision-making.

It's not surprising that people cope by being *selective* about the information – focusing on some things at the expense of others.

Large dogs should be in a secure area to the rear of a hatchback, with a screen to stop them being thrown forward in an accident.

The Highway Code advises you *not* to use your mobile if you have an accident on a motorway. Use the (free) emergency phone; it connects directly to the police, who will then be able to identify your exact location.

MOBILE PHONES

You're likely to get a question about mobile phones in your Theory Test, because the Government and the Driving Standards Agency are

becoming increasingly concerned about the potential of mobiles to distract drivers.

Research proves you are four times more likely to be involved in an accident if using a mobile phone while driving.

Therefore remember that:

- you should never use a hand-held mobile phone while driving
- and even if your phone is the hands-free kind, it can still distract you from watching the road.

Tests show that under normal circumstances experienced drivers have an improved level of hazard perception when compared with new drivers, but when they're using a mobile phone there is *no difference* between new and experienced drivers!

Remember: your hands are connected to your brain, and if your brain's occupied elsewhere, it will affect the action of your hands on the wheel.

At the time of writing it's not actually *illegal* to make a phone call on the move, but this may well change.

So, what should you do?

THE ANSWER'S SIMPLE! –

find a safe place to stop and *then* make the call!

As for *receiving* calls, the best advice is not to have the phone turned on while you're driving; or to turn on the message facility until you can stop and return the call.

FORWARD PLANNING

This is the skill that you need so that you can act on what you have observed on the road ahead.

For example:

You're coming up to a roundabout and you can see that traffic is stationary on the opposite side. By looking ahead you can work out that if you move on to the roundabout, you will block other traffic from flowing and leaving at other exits.

So, after **observing** the situation you would use your **forward planning** skills to avoid making the problem worse.

Summary

All of these key skills work together to make you a better driver.

- If you're *concentrating* on the road
- And *observing* what's happening
- You'll be able to *anticipate* possible hazards
- And *plan* your actions ahead.

Motorway driving **is where you need your forward planning skills most of all; in deciding when to overtake, signalling and moving out in good time, and anticipating hazards ahead. (See also Motorway rules, page 107.)**

ALERTNESS

There's another reason why you might not spot an approaching hazard until you're almost on top of it – it could be summed up like this:

ARE YOU FIT TO DRIVE?

'*Fit*' can mean:

- Have you had any alcoholic drinks before you set out?
- Are you under the influence of illegal substances (drugs)?
- Are you feeling groggy or unwell?
- Are you taking prescription medicine which could affect your ability to control the car?
- Are you too tired to drive?

We'll deal with drink and drugs a little later (see 'Driving under the influence', page 95).

It's unwise to set out on a journey if you're not well, on the basis of 'I'll see how I go – I'll probably be all right':

- your reactions are likely to be *slower*
- you may be *unable to judge* distances properly
- your actions may be *less well co-ordinated* than usual.

Make sure the car's ventilator fans are working efficiently, to help you stay alert.

And of course, warnings printed on the labels of prescription medicines such as

'*DO NOT DRIVE OR OPERATE MACHINERY*'

are put there for good reasons!

If you are tired and there is some distance to go to a service station, open the window for a few moments to let in some fresh air.

If you drive when you are too tired, you risk falling asleep at the wheel – an all too common cause of serious accidents. Driving for long stretches on a motorway at night can be especially dangerous. If you sense that you are losing your concentration, then *take a break*. Make use of motorway service stations to stop for a (non-alcoholic!) drink and a short walk before resuming your journey.

Plan your journey ahead, giving yourself plenty of time for **rest stops** – at least every couple of hours.

To end this section, here are some of the hazards you're likely to encounter in everyday driving, and how you might deal with them.

Hazard

Slow vehicle such as a milk float or road maintenance vehicle going up a steep hill in front of you.

Response

You can overtake, but only if:

● you can see it's safe to do so
● there are no road markings or signs prohibiting overtaking
● the road is sufficiently wide.

Hazard

Parked vehicles on your side of the road – not enough room for two cars to pass.

Response

Give way to traffic from the other direction.

Stop well behind the parked cars so that you can see clearly to move out when it's your turn.

Don't forget to watch out for pedestrians (especially children) appearing from between the cars (see page 54).

Don't forget to test your brakes as soon as you can after driving through a ford. This is because the brakes will have got wet through.

Hazard

A bus starts to pull out in front of you and you can only allow it to do so if you slam on your brakes.

Response

If driving along a road where buses operate, anticipate that they may need to pull out and allow them to do so. If you have to slam on your brakes to let the bus pull out, you're going too fast.

Hazard

The roads are icy, and it's foggy too.

Response

You need to adapt your normal driving technique to minimise the risk of accidents. Allow as much as ten times the normal distance between you and the car in front. And decide whether your journey is really necessary.

Hazard

You notice that there are tram rails on the road.

Response

Keep a sharp look out for trams – they may approach silently, and cannot steer out of the way to avoid a motorist.

Hazard

You come to a ford in the road.

Response

Drive through slowly in first gear, slipping the clutch but continuing to rev the engine; this will give you more power, and blow out water from the exhaust. Don't forget the ford could be frozen over in winter.

There are innumerable other hazards we could list here; most involve unusually large or slow vehicles, extreme weather conditions, and obstructions of one kind or another.

Your **driving test examiner** will be watching to see how you cope with them, and whether you are anticipating possible hazards.

Once you've passed your test, it's very trying to find that some other drivers don't obey the same rules:

- for example, if you've kept a good distance between you and the lorry in front so that you can see clearly to overtake, and then someone overtakes you and fills the gap!

But *stick with the driving techniques that **you** know to be right.*

TEST YOUR UNDERSTANDING OF THIS SECTION

1. What are some of the key skills you need to be a safe driver?

2. What things can distract you from concentrating on your driving?

3. What should you do if you need to make a call on your mobile phone when you're driving?

4. If the journey to your holiday destination takes about six hours, how many rest stops should you make along the way?

5. When driving in icy conditions, you need to allow extra space between you and the car in front. Is it: twice the normal distance, four times, or ten times?

Answers on page 185

It's in the rules

The most complete guide to the rules of the road is, of course, *The Highway Code.*

In it you'll find rules not just for motorists but for pedestrians, cyclists and motorcyclists as well; and rules for horses, dogs and other animals on the road.

You'll need to study *The Highway Code* in addition to a reliable guide such as the AA's *Driving Test Theory (Official Questions and Answers)* as part of your preparation for the **Theory Test**. (See also page 154.)

And when you take your **practical test**, the driving examiner will assess your knowledge of *The Highway Code* from your general driving.

What follows is a summary of some of the rules relating to:

- **crossroads**
- **junctions**
- **lanes and roundabouts**
- **pedestrian crossings and level crossings**
- **road signs and road markings**
- **speed limits**
- **stopping distances**
- **towing** (e.g. caravans, trailers)

A separate section focuses on **parking**, and another on **motorway rules**.

(*Note:* traffic signs used on motorways will be dealt with in the 'Motorway Rules' section, page 107.)

CROSSROADS

At a crossroads you'll find some of the following:

- a roundabout
- traffic lights
- road signs
- road markings (see diagram below)
- nothing at all! (see diagram bottom)

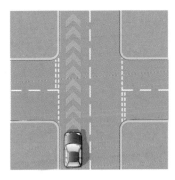

Fortunately, the last one is becoming increasingly rare, but where you do find an unmarked crossroads, it's one of the places where there is a *high risk of accidents*.

At an unmarked crossroads –
no one has priority.

So, look all around and take care before proceeding.

There are certain conventions (which people don't always observe), such as:

- If you're going straight across and there's someone opposite who wants to turn right, generally you go first.
- If you're both waiting to turn right, you're supposed to drive around each other right side to right side.

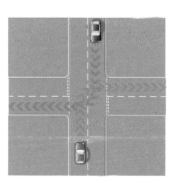

However, it's not against the law to go left side to left side – but it is more risky, as your view of oncoming vehicles will be blocked.

In other countries be prepared for different conventions; for example, Australians observe a rule called 'priority of the right' here.

If you see a traffic light sign with a diagonal red strip across it, this tells you that the lights are out of order. Interestingly, drivers will often drive much *better*, and give way to each other, when the lights aren't working!

CROSSROADS WITH TRAFFIC LIGHTS

Make sure you're quite clear on:
- the meaning of all the traffic light signals
- the sequence of colours.

Green means 'Go' – *but only if you can see that it's safe.*

Amber on its own means 'Stop'

Red means 'Stop'

Red and amber still means 'Stop'

If you can see that the road beyond the lights is still blocked by traffic, then

STAY WHERE YOU ARE! even if you have to wait for the lights to go through another sequence. *Note:* on checking whether the road beyond a crossroads or other junction is clear, see also 'Box junctions' on the next page.

TRAFFIC LIGHTS WITH GREEN ARROWS

Green arrow lights (filter lights) can be attached to either side of a set of traffic lights, or be mounted on the lights themselves. When the green arrow lights up, your way should be clear to turn in that direction; sometimes it's before and sometimes it's after the full 'green' phase.

(See 'Level crossings', page 76, for more on traffic light signals.)

BOX JUNCTIONS

These were introduced to prevent blockages at crossroads and other junctions.

The rule is:

DO NOT ENTER THE BOX UNLESS YOUR EXIT IS CLEAR.

Usually you will not stop in the yellow box unless, while your exit route is clear, you are caused to wait by oncoming traffic.

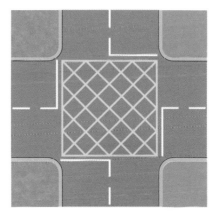

By far the greatest number of accidents occur within 18 metres (20 yards) of a junction.

JUNCTIONS

Junctions present some of the worst hazards for drivers.

T-junctions and **staggered junctions** have been shown to be far more dangerous than roundabouts, or even crossroads.

But it's worth noting that a significant number of accidents also occur at **private drives and entrances**.

How to keep accidents at junctions down to a minimum

If you're on a major road where there are junctions with minor roads:

- watch out for vehicles joining from side roads
- don't overtake when you can see there's a junction coming up on either side of the road.

If you're at a junction waiting to join a major road:

- don't proceed until you're sure it's safe. Give way to traffic on the major road.

And remember – **Mirror, Signal, Manoeuvre**.

If, when you're waiting to pull out of a side road, an approaching car on the main road indicates left:

- don't pull out until the other vehicle has actually begun to turn. The driver may suddenly change his or her mind, or the indicator may be flashing in error. Look out for vehicles following the turning car.

What to watch out for at junctions

- cyclists and motorcyclists – take care not to trap a cyclist on the inside when you're turning left.
- pedestrians – they may be crossing a road that you're turning into. *They* have priority, so don't hassle them!

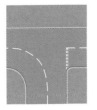    

Road markings and signs at junctions

(See also 'Follow the signs', page 77 and 'Crossing the line', page 79.)

If you're joining a major road from a minor road, the signs and road markings will clearly tell you to STOP or GIVE WAY.

At a STOP sign, you *must* come to a complete stop.

At a GIVE WAY sign, you may not have to stop completely if the road is clear.

Slip roads at junctions

Some major roads – and all motorways – will have slip roads to help you when you're joining.

BUT YOU SHOULD STILL GIVE WAY –

rather than shooting ahead to join the major road by overtaking on the left!

See 'Motorway rules', page 109, for information about overtaking on the left when on a motorway.

Remember to acknowledge courtesy from other drivers; it encourages them to do it again!

The only times it's OK to 'overtake' on the left are: when the vehicle in front is signalling to turn right, and there is room for you to pass on the left; in queues on a motorway when a lane to the right is temporarily moving faster; and in a one-way street.

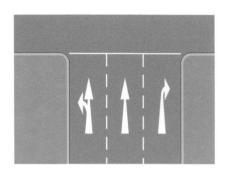

GET IN LANE

A road sign telling you to do this can strike terror into the heart of a novice motorist –

'Am I in the right lane?'

'What do I do if I'm not?'

'Will I have time to move to the lane I need to be in?'

This is yet another occasion when using your *anticipation* skills is vital.

How to deal with lanes

If you're looking well ahead, you should have plenty of time to select the correct lane for your destination and to move into it – *having first checked that it's safe to do so*, by using **Mirror, Signal, Manoeuvre.**

And if you *do* make a mistake –

DON'T PANIC!

Simply:

- control your speed
- indicate
- transfer to the correct lane in good time, and when there is enough space.

Note: if it's clear that you've left it too late to make the change safely, you should continue in the same lane and find another route to your destination.

Lanes are most frequently found:

- in towns and cities, especially where one-way systems operate
- on dual carriageways and motorways
- on the approaches to roundabouts
- at traffic lights.

LANES AND ROUNDABOUTS

As you come up to a roundabout:

- use progressive braking
- select the lane you want to be in
- use your indicators to signal if you intend to turn left or right.

IF YOU'RE TAKING THE EXIT LEADING TO THE ROAD AHEAD –

- don't indicate as you approach, but indicate left as you pass the exit before the one you plan to take.

Remember, on a roundabout the rule is always:

- *give way to traffic from the right.*

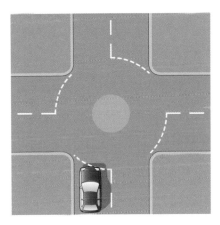

Although you're concentrating on positioning your car correctly, you'll find that there are some types of road users who seem to be doing something different.

Vehicles not playing by the rules at roundabouts

Part of your hazard awareness is to know that there are some vehicles that don't keep to the normal lane when approaching a roundabout. This is due to their large size, or vulnerability on the road.

- **Cyclists** sometimes stay in the left lane while giving an arm signal indicating that they want to turn right. *Slow down* and give them room to move across.

In your driving test, where there are lanes the examiner will check your position on the road; it's important not to be straddling two at a time.

- The same applies to **horse riders**.
- **Long vehicles** may need to begin their right turn by taking up part of the left lane. *Stay well back and give them room to manoeuvre.*

Of course – incorrect road positioning may also just be down to bad driving!

LANE CLOSURES

These are a frequent feature of **motorways** (see page 110), but are also found on other major roads such as dual carriageways.

They are generally found where there are **road-works**.

You'll usually get *plenty of warning* of a lane closure: *traffic signs* will be put up well ahead, and part of the road may be *coned off* before the area of road-works.

So – *change lanes in good time.*

It's likely that a *temporary speed limit* will be in operation, so be prepared to drive at a slower speed than is usual for that road.

Sometimes the whole carriageway is closed, with a sign indicating you should cross to the opposite one.

This is called a *contraflow*. Points to remember here are:

- drive even more carefully, as you'll have to keep in very narrow lanes
- stay in the lane you're in.

STAY IN LANE

Max speed 30

OTHER TYPES OF LANES

Bus lanes

Bus lanes are marked on the road, and usually by signs as well.

Some bus lanes only operate at certain times of the day.

- You're not allowed to drive (or park!) in a bus lane during its hours of operation, or to move into one in order to overtake.

Note: the same rules apply to **tram lanes**.

- In one-way systems, bus lanes often run *in the opposite direction to the rest of the traffic;* this is sometimes true of cycle lanes too.
- If you want to turn left and there is a bus lane or tram lane in operation, *give way* to buses or trams – whichever direction they're coming from.

Cycle lanes

Cycle lanes are marked by signs and by a white line along the road.
If it's a *solid* white line –

> it means don't drive or park in it during its times of operation.

If it's a *broken* white line –

> you can only drive or park in it if there is no alternative, and not at any time when waiting restrictions apply (see 'Where to park – and where not to', page 92).

In some instances cyclists can use the bus lane, if the sign has symbols for both.

PEDESTRIAN CROSSINGS

(See also 'I didn't even see him', page 52.)

There are some general rules that apply to all types of pedestrian crossings.

- *Don't overtake* a vehicle that's slowing down as it approaches a crossing.
- *Don't harass pedestrians* who might be a bit slow, by revving your engine or edging the car forward or any other method.
- As you approach any pedestrian crossing, *slow down and be prepared to stop*.

Zebra crossings

A zebra crossing isn't controlled by pedestrian lights, but usually there's an orange flashing beacon.

The rule here is that you must stop and give way to pedestrians once a person has stepped on to the crossing. Also be prepared for somebody pushing a pram in front of them.

Pelican crossings

These *are* controlled by lights:
- red for 'STOP' followed by
- flashing amber.

When the amber light is flashing, give way to pedestrians already on the crossing.

Toucan and puffin crossings

These are like pelican crossings, but without the 'flashing' phase.

At toucan crossings, cyclists are allowed to ride across.

Pegasus crossings

In some parts of the UK you'll find pegasus crossings, which are designed for horse riders; they can press the button without dismounting. If you notice a sign for a pegasus crossing, this alerts you to watch out for horses.

One crossing or two?

At **zebra** crossings where there's an island in the centre, pedestrians should treat it as two crossings, and wait half-way across the road.

Pelican crossings that go straight across the road count as one crossing even if there's a central island, so you must wait for pedestrians who've started to cross from the other side of the road – *even if the signal for drivers has changed to flashing amber or green by the time they get half-way*.

Staggered crossings

However, if the crossings on either side of the central island are *not* in a straight line, they count as *two separate crossings* and the pedestrians have to press the button a second time when they're half-way across, and wait for the green light or figure.

At crossings, where motorists see a red traffic light, pedestrians usually see a green figure (walking), and where motorists see a flashing amber light, pedestrians usually see a flashing green figure.

Similar lights and warning sounds operate at some hospital entrances and ambulance stations, at swing bridges, and within airport boundaries.

LEVEL CROSSINGS

These come in so many different types that two pages in *The Highway Code* are devoted to them; you should study these pages carefully.

Most crossings have *warning lights*, *alarm sounds* and *barriers*; but there are some level crossings with no barriers, and crossing these demands great caution. The signs for these are shown below.

Some have gates you operate yourself; there is normally a phone to use before you proceed.

At crossings with automatic barriers:

● Don't try to speed up to get across as the barrier comes down, or attempt to zigzag around half-barriers.

● If the barrier stays down after the train's gone, it means there's another train coming.

● If you're driving a large vehicle, use the telephone provided before starting to cross.

What if your car breaks down half-way across?

● get all the passengers out and tell them to move away from the crossing

● if there's a railway phone, use it to alert the signal operator

● attempt to move your vehicle, *but only if there's time before the train comes.*

FOLLOW THE SIGNS

Road and traffic signs come in three main shapes:

- **circular**, like this 'No entry' sign

- **triangular**, like this sign for a staggered junction

- and **rectangular**, like this direction sign on a main road.

Circles – are for giving orders

Triangles – are for giving warnings

Rectangles – are for giving information

In addition,

*SIGNS WITH RED CIRCLES USUALLY GIVE ORDERS **NOT TO DO** SOMETHING*

and

*SIGNS WITH BLUE CIRCLES GIVE INSTRUCTIONS **TO DO** SOMETHING*

You'll find a set of the more commonly used road signs printed in your copy of *The Highway Code*.

Although *The Highway Code* shows modern versions of the signs, you may find more old-fashioned signs still in use in some places.

Did you know? There's one sign which is octagonal: the 'STOP' sign. This is to make it stand out more.

When you come to a junction the examiner may ask you to make a turn; but you're expected to watch out for lane markings on the road and signs giving directions, and to make decisions about how to react to these yourself.

ROAD SIGNS AND YOUR DRIVING TEST

When you take your practical driving test, you should be able to demonstrate by your driving that you know and understand all the signs and road markings along the route.

You'll be expected to look ahead and be *aware* of them in advance (see 'Anticipation', page 53) so that you can react to them in good time.

When you take your **Theory Test**, you're likely to find questions on one or more of these:

- the different sign shapes
- the meanings of individual signs
- what sorts of signs to expect at certain road systems (such as a one-way street, or a contraflow)
- how you should react when you see a particular sign.

But however differently the questions are worded – it all comes down to how well you know *The Highway Code*.

CROSSING THE LINE

A guide to white lines and other road markings.

White lines can be found on the road going at different angles:

- across the road (telling you to stop, give way etc.)
- along the road (indicating the centre, or dividing the road into lanes etc.).

Lines across the road

(These are used in conjunction with road signs, see page 77.) As a general rule, more paint on the road signals more danger.

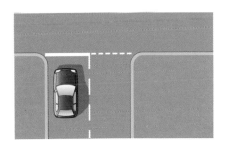

A **single continuous** white line across the road in front of you means STOP.

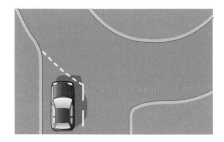

A **single broken** white line is used at roundabouts to indicate 'give way to traffic from the right'. It is also found at the end of the slip roads to dual carriageways and motorways.

A **double broken** white line will be found where you're joining a major road from a minor road, and means 'give way to traffic on major road'.

Since the lines are double, they remind you to take extra care and to *look out for hazards*.

A 'STOP' line with a 'STOP' sign is thicker than a 'STOP' line at signals.

The broken white line used for mini-roundabouts looks slightly different from that at a normal junction.

When the
line becomes
longer with
shorter gaps, it
means *there's
a hazard ahead.*

Lines along the road

A **single white line** along the **edge** of
the road is just that – it marks the
edge.

Other lines along the edge may be
yellow or even red, and are generally
connected with **parking** (see pages
90–94).

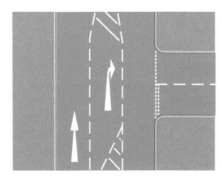

Broken white lines

A **broken white line** is used to mark
the centre of the road.

ONLY CROSS IT

when

- you can see that the road is clear,
  so you move out to overtake a
  slow vehicle

or

- when you turn right off the road.

In the diagram, left, hatched
markings in the middle of the main
road allow you a waiting space when
turning right, in addition to the
broken white lines.

Double white lines where the one nearest to you is a broken line and the other a solid line

This means you can cross the line, for example to overtake – as long as you can see far enough ahead to complete the manoeuvre before another solid white line starts on your side.

Double white lines

The general rule is don't cross where the lines are double – it won't be safe to do so.

*When **can** you cross the lines?*

- in an emergency
- if turning right
- if you have to pass a stationary vehicle
- if you have to overtake a horse and rider, a slow-moving road maintenance vehicle, or a cyclist. But they must be travelling at 10mph or less.

Look out for curved white arrows on the road – these are put there to remind you to *get back on your side!*

The 30mph limit also applies to unclassified roads in Scotland.

SPEED LIMITS

The rule is:

KEEP TO THE SPEED LIMIT SHOWN FOR –

- the road you're on

and

- the vehicle you're driving.

It's safe to assume the limit will be 30mph in a built-up area, and anywhere where there are street lights.

The speed limits shown in the table opposite are *maximum* speeds.

Weather conditions, night driving, driving behind cyclists or motorcyclists, and adjusting for bends in the road will all have an effect on your speed –

so you'll very often be *below the limit* where speed is concerned.

KNOW YOUR LIMITS

Type of vehicle	Built-up area	Single carriageways	Dual carriageways	Motorways
Cars & motorcycles (including car-derived vans up to 2 tonnes maximum laden weight)	30mph	60mph	70mph	70mph
Cars towing caravans or trailers (including car-derived vans and motorcycles)	30mph	50mph	60mph	60mph
Buses & coaches (not exceeding 12 metres in overall length)	30mph	50mph	60mph	70mph
Goods vehicles (not exceeding 7.5 tonnes maximum laden weight)	30mph	50mph	60mph	70mph*
Goods vehicles (exceeding 7.5 tonnes maximum laden weight)	30mph	40mph	50mph	60mph

*Limited to **60mph** if articulated or towing a trailer

Don't forget that motor-cycles and large vehicles may have longer stopping distances than cars.

STOPPING DISTANCES

It's worth spending a bit of time getting your head round this, since you are likely to be asked questions about stopping distances in your Theory Test.

Remember:

YOUR STOPPING DISTANCE IS MADE UP OF YOUR THINKING DISTANCE + YOUR BRAKING DISTANCE.

It's not unknown for Theory Test candidates to protest that they were marked wrong on a question they thought they'd got right – because they weren't clear about the differences between *Thinking Distance – Braking Distance – and Overall Stopping Distance.*

What are stopping distances tables meant to do?

Although you have to 'learn' them to pass your Theory test, it's important to understand their purpose.

You'll build up experience while driving of how much space you need to leave between you and the car in front so that, if need be, you could stop suddenly if that vehicle did the same. However, so that **you don't build up that experience by means of a series of 'near-misses'**, the table opposite gives a good guide.

overall stopping distance 23m

30mph →   **thinking 9m** | **braking 14m** |

KNOW WHEN TO STOP

Speed	Thinking distance	Braking distance	Overall stopping distance
20mph	6 metres (20 feet)	6 metres (20 feet)	12 metres (40 feet) or 3 car lengths
30mph	9 metres (30 feet)	14 metres (45 feet)	23 metres (75 feet) or 6 car lengths
40mph	12 metres) (40 feet	24 metres (80 feet)	36 metres (120 feet) or 9 car lengths
50mph	15 metres (50 feet)	38 metres (125 feet)	53 metres (175 feet) or 13 car lengths
60mph	18 metres (60 feet)	55 metres (180 feet)	73 metres (240 feet) or 18 car lengths
70mph	21 metres (70 feet)	75 metres (245 feet)	96 metres (315 feet) or 24 car lengths

Note: an average car length is 4 metres (13 feet).

If you have to park your vehicle on the roadside overnight with a trailer attached, it must have lights. Unattached trailers need lights too.

TOWING

Your trailer should be of a suitable size to match your car – ideally, it should weigh no more than 85% of the car's weight. This is your car's **MTC** – Maximum Towing Capacity. When you're towing a trailer, you need to be aware of the following points:

- The trailer must be fitted with brakes.
- It's safer to stay well *below* the maximum weight, because a vehicle such as a caravan has a high *volume* compared with its *mass*.
- If you plan to tow a trailer that has no brakes, the trailer should weigh *no more than half* of the weight of your vehicle. The *maximum* weight for a trailer without brakes is 750kg.

MAM and GTW

MAM stands for Maximum Authorised Mass. This means the maximum that any vehicle can weigh, taking into account the weight of passengers and other loads.

GTW stands for Gross Train Weight; nothing to do with railways, but referring to the maximum weight that it's safe for a particular vehicle to handle. The GTW is calculated from the weight of vehicle (including its load) added to the weight of any trailer it's towing and that trailer's load.

You must not tow any load that would cause your vehicle to become unsafe. When the MAM is at full capacity with passengers, roof rack etc., the car may not have enough GTW for you to be able to tow the maximum size of trailer for your car's MTC.

General guidelines

- Check your driving licence; it will tell you how much you're allowed to tow.
- Check your car manual for how much the manufacturer recommends you to tow, and *never exceed* the manufacturer's limit.
- Don't overload either your car or your trailer.
- Make sure the load is secure.
- Make sure that none of it sticks out in a dangerous manner.

Tow bars

Take care, if you're buying a trailer, that it fits your car's tow bar.

A tow bar has to include one or more seven-pin sockets to connect to the *lights* on the trailer.

Note: tow bars now have to conform to EU regulations.

More about towing

For information about the difference a trailer makes to the way your vehicle handles, see 'Motorway do's and don't's', page 108, and 'Shift that load!', page 137. You also need to adjust your speed, see page 138.

Did you know? By law the driver must be able to tell that the indicators on the trailer are working properly. A flashing light inside the car does the job.

TEST YOUR UNDERSTANDING OF THIS SECTION

1. When two vehicles are approaching an unmarked crossroads, which one has priority?

2. For what reason could you decide to wait in a box junction before your exit is clear?

3. You're turning left on to a main road from a side road, and you can see a car approaching from the right and indicating left. How can you be sure that the road is clear for you to proceed?

4. What shape of road marking means 'Give Way'?

5. What action should you take if you realise you're in the wrong lane?

6. What is the key rule to remember at roundabouts?

7. At what times, if any, are you allowed to drive in a cycle lane marked by a solid white line?

8. Do you have to stop at a zebra crossing if a pedestrian has not actually put their foot on it?

9. What shape would you expect a road sign to be if it is giving an order?

10. How is a hazard warning line on the road different from a 'normal' white line?

11. If you're driving in a road where there are street lights, it's usual for the speed limit to be?

12. Is there any difference in the national speed limits for single carriageway roads and dual carriageways?

13. Should you drive more slowly than normal when you're towing a caravan?

14. Is it good driving practice to drive at the maximum speed allowed by the speed limit for the road you're on?

15. How much weight is it legal for a car to tow?

Answers on page 186–7

You can't park there!

Leave extra space if you park near a vehicle which is displaying a Blue Card (formerly the Orange Badge). This indicates that the driver is disabled, and may need more room to manoeuvre. (See 'Where to park – and where not to', page 93.)

Parking is a subject which causes a great deal of aggravation, to drivers, pedestrians and home-owners alike; and as more and more cars appear on our roads, the problems associated with parking just seem to get worse.

The question to keep in mind is –

- will I be breaking the law, or causing inconvenience or danger to anyone, if I decide to park in a particular place?

As the title of this section implies, it's easier to list the places where you *can't* park than those where you *can!*

You'll find a summary of forbidden parking places on pages 92–3. But first, assuming you succeed in finding a parking place on the road, here are a few points to remember.

- Park as close as you can to the kerb, and parallel to it.
- Don't leave the car with its wheels half-on and half-off the kerb.

- Leave just enough space for your car and others to get in and out comfortably. Take care not to block others in, and don't take up more than one space.
- Before you leave the car, check that you've put the handbrake on.
- Also check that the engine is turned off, and all lights are switched off – unless it's at night and you're in an area where you need to leave sidelights on (see 'Parking at night', page 93). You also have to leave the sidelights on if you're parking a trailer overnight (see 'Towing', page 86).
- When leaving the car, check your door mirror and over your shoulder before you open the door carefully, so that you don't hit a passing vehicle or pedestrian.
- Lock the vehicle when you leave it.

PARKING AND YOUR DRIVING TEST

Your driving instructor will give you tuition in how to position the car when parking.

As part of your test, you will have to carry out a reversing manoeuvre (see 'Reversing', page 19).

You'll be expected to be able to reverse into a space behind a parked car; or into a marked parking bay; and to end up with the wheels straight if possible. The diagram, right, shows the correct position for your car on the road as you reverse into a parking space between two vehicles.

While you're reversing:
- keep looking all around for pedestrians and other vehicles
- make good use of your mirrors
- stay in control of the car the whole time.

This manoeuvre is of course easier if your car's got power-assisted steering, but with regular practice your parking technique will improve whatever car you drive.

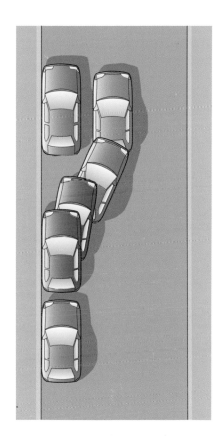

Remember – *take your time when reversing,* **and don't be hurried by what you imagine other drivers might be thinking about you!**

The sign for a clearway is a red cross in a red circle, on a blue background.

WHERE TO PARK – AND WHERE NOT TO

When driving in town it's sensible to use:

- purpose-built car parks
- parking meter zones
- park-and-ride schemes.

Finding parking places out of town is generally easier, but you may still encounter restrictions (such as residents' parking schemes) – and some country lanes are just too narrow to park in safely.

Where you *know* that parking is likely to be a problem, it's better to use public transport, or to walk or cycle instead (while gaining environmental 'brownie points' at the same time!).

Deciding where to park

Always look for **traffic signs** or **road markings** indicating that you shouldn't park. Here are some of the common 'no-go' areas for parking:

- any part of a motorway – this includes the hard shoulder, and motorway approach roads (slip roads). When on a motorway, the service areas are the only safe places to park.
- any road which is a 'clearway'
- bus, cycle or tram lanes during their hours of operation (see page 73)

- pedestrian crossings and the approaches to them (marked by zigzag lines on the road)
- approaches to level crossings (see page 76).

As well as road signs, a large number of **markings along the edge of the road** are used to indicate 'No Waiting'.

You'll find all these in your *Highway Code*.

Yellow lines may allow you to load or unload goods or passengers at certain times.

Red lines (single or double) are found in London and mean 'No Stopping'.

Get to know these different road markings, and look out for them when you're out driving or on foot.

Other places not to park

- at a bus stop
- at the entrance to a school
- across a driveway
- in a space reserved for Blue Card holders
- obstructing entrances and exits used by emergency services
- opposite or within 10 metres (32 feet) of a junction
- on the brow of a hill
- on a bend.

Four cars in the diagram below are parked illegally or inconsiderately – can you spot which ones?

PARKING AT NIGHT

There are some extra rules about parking at night.

- Don't park the wrong way round – that is, facing the opposite way to the flow of traffic.
- Park with sidelights on if in an area where the speed limit is over 30mph.
- As already mentioned, any vehicle towing a trailer that's parked overnight must have lights showing (see page 86).

- It's OK to park on the right in a one-way street at night.

PARKING ON A HILL

If you have to park on a hill, leave the car 'in gear', as follows:

- if you're facing *up hill*, put the car in a *forward gear*.
- if you're facing *down hill*, put the car in *reverse gear*.

Turn the wheels towards the side of the road, unless you are parked on a road with a kerb, and facing up hill, when you should turn the wheels *away* from the kerb. (For an automatic car, use 'Park' as normal.)

You may have seen a driver park and rush into a house or shop saying 'I've left the engine running'. You should *never* do this, as it's both illegal *and* highly dangerous.

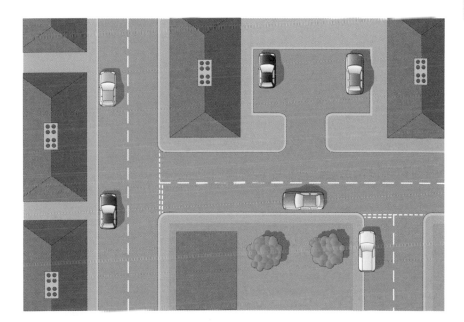

TEST YOUR UNDERSTANDING
OF THIS SECTION

1. How should you position your car when parking in the street?

2. Where should you look for places to park in town centres?

3. Can you park in a 'Disabled' space in a car park if you are quite sure all the other spaces are full?

4. Do you need to leave your sidelights on when parking at night?

5. What extra precautions should you take if you have to park on a hill?

Answers on page 188

Driving under the influence

Where alcohol and drugs are concerned, there's a short answer to all questions about whether to drive while under the influence –

DON'T!

ALCOHOL

Young people are perhaps more enlightened than their elders about the dangers of drinking and driving; especially if they have had personal experience of being in a road accident, or if a friend has been killed or badly hurt.

Many of these young people make a very sensible decision when they're going out in a group: the nominated driver doesn't drink alcohol during the evening.

But for people with no direct experience of road accidents, it's quite easy to be unaware of their devastating effects. Perhaps it's because our world is tuned in to TV images, and what we don't see on TV, we don't find worrying. We're shown horrifying images of children and young people injured in wars in other countries, and of course we don't find their misery acceptable. But we don't usually see similarly shocking pictures of road accident victims in our own country, and so the size of the problem stays hidden.

Here are a few statistics:
- Road accidents cost us £15 billion per year
- Three and a half thousand people die in road accidents every year
- 300,000 are injured every year.

ASKING THE WRONG QUESTIONS

So, the aim of this section *isn't* to answer the questions

> 'How much can I have to drink and still be under the limit?'
> *or*
> 'How can I drink and drive and avoid being caught?'

However, here's some information for reference.

Most drink-driving accidents happen during *short journeys*; 70% happen *within the first three miles* of the journey.

If you were to drive when you were more than twice over the limit, you'd be *at least 50 times* more likely to have an accident.

- At present, the police in the UK don't have the power to carry out random breath tests.
- A police officer can ask you to take a breath test if he or she has reasonable cause to believe you've been drinking and driving; or if you've committed a traffic offence.
- Drivers at accident scenes are breathalysed as a matter of routine.

The legal limits are:
- 35 milligrams of alcohol in 100 millilitres of breath

or
- 80 milligrams of alcohol in 100 millilitres of blood

or
- 107 milligrams of alcohol in 100 millilitres of urine.

You may also hear the blood alcohol level described as 'point eight'; in other countries it's often as low as 'point five'.

How many pints is that?

It would be risky to say how many pints of beer or glasses of wine make up the legal limit, because the effects of the same size drink can vary considerably from person to person. You may be affected much more quickly if you drink alcohol

on an empty stomach, or if you're not well.
- It's not possible to bring down your alcohol level by drinking coffee.
- If you have a drink at lunchtime, you probably still won't be safe to drive by the evening.
- The same applies to drinking in the evening and driving the following morning.

The **penalties** for driving under the influence of alcohol are listed in full in *The Highway Code*; serious drink-driving offences will always result in being **disqualified from driving** for 18 months or more.

The **cost of insuring your car** will also go up if you have a drink-driving conviction.

However:

All of the information available about drinking and driving *isn't* negative.

Recent surveys show that far fewer drivers now see drinking and driving as an acceptable risk, compared with 20 years ago.

DRUGS

All of the risks associated with driving after drinking alcohol are, of course, equally associated with driving under the influence of drugs.

- You may become unreasonably confident about your skill as a driver, and take more risks.
- Your co-ordination will be affected and your reactions will be slower than normal.
- Your hazard awareness will be diminished.
- You will be less accurate when judging distance, and the speed of other vehicles.

It's more difficult to assess the effects of drugs than the effects of alcohol – *they may well be stronger*.

But –

WHAT ABOUT DRUGS PRESCRIBED BY YOUR DOCTOR?

This is a very important issue, and you'll find a large number of questions about it in the DSA's bank of Theory Test questions (regularly updated, and available in an AA book).

When you are taking prescription medicines:

- Pay attention to information or warnings about driving given on the label (see 'Alertness', page 60).
- Check with your doctor or pharmacist about whether the medicine prescribed will affect your ability to drive safely.
- A common side effect of some medicines (e.g. cough medicines) is to make you feel drowsy. Tiredness is one of the most frequent causes of accidents (see 'Alertness', page 60) – and it's one of the reasons to take extra care when **driving at night**.

The next section deals with the particular hazards you can encounter in night driving.

About half of people killed in night-time road accidents are found to have been above the legal limit for alcohol.

TEST YOUR UNDERSTANDING
OF THIS SECTION

1. Are the police within their rights
   to stop you and ask you to take a
   breath test?

2. When going out for an evening
   with friends, what can you do to
   avoid being caught for drink-
   driving?

3. If you drink alcohol in the
   evening, is there any reason why
   you should not drive the
   following morning?

4. What are the main effects of drugs
   and alcohol on your driving
   ability?

5. Would it be safe to drive after
   taking some cough medicine, if
   the doctor has prescribed it for
   you personally?

Answers on page 189

It's different at night

If you learn to drive in the winter, you may have some lessons in the dark; but if not, you can take and pass your test without having much idea about how to adjust your driving technique for **driving at night**.

On the one hand:

- headlights can give you more warning of oncoming traffic than you would get in the day

but on the other hand:

- hazards are more difficult to see in the dark

- pedestrians may behave more erratically – for example, at closing time for pubs – and they may not *all* be wearing light coloured clothing as recommended in *The Highway Code*, still less reflective armbands!

- if you haven't kept your screenwash filled up and replaced faulty wipers (see 'Look after your car...', pages 38–9), your windscreen will become impossible to see through in the dark due to grease smears etc.

- your field of vision is generally

A recent survey showed that 7 out of 10 motorists are afraid of driving in the dark.

Did you know that it's **illegal** to drive with faulty lights? Carry spares and fuses – in some countries this is a legal requirement.

Use dipped headlights in the day as well, whenever it's gloomy and/or raining.

narrower than in daylight

- you run the risk of being dazzled by the headlights of an oncoming car if they are badly adjusted, or deliberately too bright (see 'How am I driving?', page 114).

You'll need to make allowances for the increased risks. So:

- Check that your **lights** are all working properly.
- Drive more slowly than the maximum speed limit.
- Watch out for cyclists and pedestrians.

LIGHTING UP THE NIGHT

Sidelights

Your sidelights (and the lights on the rear registration plate) should always be on at night.

Headlights

Headlights are also necessary on most roads. Your copy of *The Highway Code* tells you where you could, theoretically, drive just on sidelights, but in practice most of the time for night driving you'll be using **dipped headlights**.

Full beam headlights are only used for country driving, where there are no street lights, and should be turned off whenever another vehicle comes into view ahead of you or is approaching on the opposite carriageway. (See 'I'm right behind you!', page 118.)

Fog lights

In normal night-time conditions there's no need to switch these on; only use them in poor visibility (100 meters or less), and switch them off again as soon as visibility improves. The unnecessary use of over-bright fog lights is an increasing symptom of driver aggression (see 'I'm right behind you!', as above).

FRONT FOG LIGHTS ARE NOT A FASHION STATEMENT!

Turn back to 'Look after your car', pages 33–4, and remind yourself of the **legal requirements** for headlights and fog lights. The alignment of your headlights will be checked as part of your car's MOT test.

TEST YOUR UNDERSTANDING OF THIS SECTION

1. Why should you take even more care when driving at night?

2. When should you use dipped headlights?

3. Is it correct to use full beam headlights when driving on a motorway?

4. When are fog lights necessary?

5. What is the effect of night driving on your field of vision?

Answers on page 190

Stormy weather

Remember the two-second rule (see 'Motorists with attitude', page 46)? Well, you can 'Say it again, When driving in rain'! In other words, you need to allow *at least twice the distance* for braking and stopping in wet weather.

Just as for night driving, you need to adjust your driving technique for different weather conditions.

If there's been a sudden downpour there may be water covering the road surface, making it difficult to control the car; and excessive speed may result in 'aquaplaning': rather like skidding, but on water, because the tyres cannot grip effectively. In order not to slide gracefully into the car in front –

KEEP YOUR DISTANCE!

DRIVING ON ICY ROADS

Ice on the road is one of the most treacherous conditions you'll encounter; the best advice is not to drive unless it's really necessary, but if you *must* make the journey –

- Allow plenty of room between you and other vehicles; your stopping distance in these conditions is at least *ten times* more than usual.
- Drive slowly; but *in as high a gear as possible* (to make your progress smoother).
- Accelerate carefully.
- Use progressive braking.
- Be very careful when steering round bends.

Conditions can change suddenly from one stretch of road to the next, and you may hit a patch of **black ice** without warning. One clue that this has happened is that your wheels will make almost no sound.

However careful you try to be, you may have to cope with a **skid** at some stage when driving in icy conditions (see page 104).

DRIVING IN SNOW

Once again, the best advice is DON'T unless you really have to.

If you must, then get yourself kitted out with emergency supplies and rescue gear including:

- a spade
- blankets or extra coats
- practical footwear (in case you have to walk some distance)
- some food and hot drinks.

In some countries, special snow tyres and snow chains (that fit around the tyres) are compulsory in winter.

All this might sound a bit over the top, but if you break down in freezing weather and have to wait for help to arrive…

Before you start

Clear ice and snow from windows, mirrors and number plate before you get moving, and make sure the lights aren't obscured by ice or grime.

Don't start driving until your front and rear screens are fully demisted.

It's illegal to start driving while your car has any snow left on it; this is because when the car warms up, the snow can block your field of vision, or dazzle you, as it slides off.

On the road

It's quite possible for road markings to get covered up by snow; and you may not be too sure where the edge of the road is. If in doubt – GIVE WAY! (This also applies when driving in fog – see page 105.)

Note: in snow, motorcyclists may take advantage of the tracks formed by cars and drive along them; this may cause them to take up a different position on the road from normal.

Remember that in older cars, having lots of the electrical features switched on at the same time (such as lights, rear window heater) can cause the car to stall when you start the engine. When you re-start the engine, switch off all non-essential equipment. Once the engine is running, let it warm up before you switch the extras back on.

SKID PAN

The main causes of skids is the driver, who either brakes too hard, accelerates fiercely or steers harshly.

ON THE SKIDS

The technique for dealing with skids can take a bit of learning at first.

For a **rear-wheel skid**:

Unless your car has ABS (see below), take your foot off the brake so that the wheels are free to turn, and re-apply immediately. At the same time, if the skid is nsot in a straight line, *steer in the same direction as the skid* to regain control.

Anti-Lock Braking System (ABS)

Because skidding occurs when the wheels lose their grip on the road surface, ABS gives no advantage once the car has gone into a skid. However, ABS will allow you to steer the car on slippery surfaces, because it applies and releases the brakes to maximum effect without locking the wheels; all you have to do is keep your foot firmly on the brake pedal.

DRIVING IN FOG

Driving in fog is always hazardous. Some techniques are more effective than others.

- *Slow down* as you drive into the fog – but remember to check your mirror first.
- Don't stick too closely behind the vehicle in front. You need to have room to stop safely if necessary. *Remember:* double the two-second rule.
- Use **dipped headlights and rear foglights** if visibility is down to 100m or less, and use **front fog lights**, if you have them – and if they give the best visibility.
- Keep your screen clear with the wipers and demisters.

If you have to negotiate a junction in dense fog, this is one of the times when it's a good idea to use your horn (see 'Sound that horn', page 119).

Once the fog has cleared, remember to switch the fog lights off, as they will dazzle other drivers when conditions are normal (see page 118).

For advice on motorway driving in fog, see the next section.

You might see a sign warning of 'FOG' when there's none to be seen – but it could be just around the corner!

Fog muffles the noise from the engine, which is one way that you can tell how fast you're going. Also, new drivers can be too nervous to take their eyes off the road to check their speed in fog.

TEST YOUR UNDERSTANDING OF THIS SECTION

1. How should you adjust your braking and stopping distances for wet or icy conditions?

2. How should you deal with skidding on an icy road?

3. What precautions do you need to take when driving in snow?

4. In fog, is it best to stay close to the vehicle in front so that you can follow their rear lights?

5. What should you always do when you see that the fog has cleared?

Answers on page 191

Motorway rules

Learner drivers aren't allowed on motorways, so you can't get experience of what it's like to drive on them until you've passed your test – although some dual carriageways now come fairly close to motorway conditions.

However, you *do* need to know all about motorway rules before taking your test, and your Theory Test will most likely include a question about motorways.

If you learn to drive with a reputable driving school you should be offered the chance of a lesson in motorway driving with your instructor. **It makes sense to take up this opportunity.**

In addition, *the new driving test* prepares you better than in previous years for coping with fast roads. Revised routes are used in the test incorporating stretches of *higher-speed roads* (where possible), giving learners a more realistic understanding of the hazards of everyday driving. This has been made possible by making the new test *seven minutes longer* than the old one.

Although your first venture on to a motorway might seem daunting, motorways are actually surprisingly safe roads. Only about 4% of accidents occur on motorways, compared with the 70% that happen in built-up areas.

The outside lane of a motorway can't be used by: vehicles pulling trailers, goods vehicles weighing over 7.5 tonnes, and passenger vehicles over 7.5 tonnes or over 12 metres in length, or adapted to carry more than 8 passengers plus the driver.

MOTORWAY 'DO'S AND DON'TS'

DO –

- Carry out **all regular checks** on your vehicle before starting a long motorway journey (see 'Safety first', page 14).
- Join the motorway by building up your speed while on the slip road to match the flow of traffic in the left-hand lane, then use **MSM**.
- *Give way* to traffic already on the motorway when joining from a slip road.
- Make use of your mirrors frequently, and look well ahead, before you move to another lane to overtake or to leave the motorway. *Check over your shoulder* for blind spots.
- *Take breaks* to avoid tiredness or falling asleep at the wheel.
- Observe **special signs** ordering lower speed limits due to bad weather or road-works (see 'Traffic signs', page 110).
- Keep to the **left** lane except when overtaking, and *return to it* once it's safe to do so.

Be aware that although the general rule is to stay in the **left-hand lane**, there are times when you need to stay in the centre lane for a while; e.g. when a line of slow-moving vehicles are moving along the left lane on an upwards gradient.

Stay in the centre lane till you have passed the hazard, then *signal* if necessary and return to the left.

DON'T –

- *REVERSE* –
  PARK –
  WALK –
  or *drive the wrong way* along the motorway!
- Exceed the **speed limit** (check the table on page 83).
- *Accelerate to a dangerous speed* when joining from a slip road.
- Allow yourself to be influenced by surrounding motorists to *drive faster than you intend*. Drive at a speed where you know you are in control (as long as it's not so slow that you become a hazard to other drivers).
- *Overtake on the left*. The only time when you can appear to 'overtake' on the left is when traffic is moving **slowly** in all three lanes, and the left lane is moving faster than the one to the right for a while.

- *Weave in and out* of the lanes of traffic.
- *Cut in sharply* after you overtake.
- Get out and pick up anything that falls from your car on to the road – *stop at the next emergency phone* and tell the police what has happened.

Posts on the edge of the motorway (see below) show the way to the nearest emergency phone.

For all other information relating to motorway driving, see your copy of *The Highway Code*.

**Remember –
when contacting
the police and
emergency
services from a
motorway,
use the phone
provided which
connects
directly to them
and identifies
your location;
always use this
in preference
to your mobile
phone (see
'Mobile
phones', page
58).**

The first sign-board, a mile before the exit, will only provide the road numbers and sometimes major town names. The half-mile sign gives major town names. Make sure you know in advance which junction number you're looking for.

TRAFFIC SIGNS AND ROAD MARKINGS ON MOTORWAYS

Light signals

In your *Highway Code* you'll find the light signals only seen on motorways. Signs above the roadway, or on the central reservation, are activated as needed, to warn of accidents, lane closures or weather conditions.

Overhead gantries display arrows or red crosses showing which lanes are open or closed to traffic, and which lanes to move to when motorways merge or diverge.

They may also show temporary speed limits.

Direction signs

Direction signs on motorways are blue and those on other major roads are green – other direction signs are white with black print.

OTHER MOTORWAY SIGNS

Reflective studs

It's useful to know the colours of studs on a motorway; this can help in working out which part of the road you're on if it's dark or foggy.

White studs mark lanes or the centre of the road

Red studs mark the left edge of the carriageway

Amber studs are used alongside the central reservation

Green studs mark the entry to a slip road.

Note: these markings are also found on some dual carriageways.

USING THE HARD SHOULDER IN AN EMERGENCY

If you can tell there's a problem developing with your vehicle while on the motorway, turn off at the next exit, or pull in to a service area.

If that's not possible, you'll have to stop your car on the hard shoulder.

- Stop as far to the left as possible, and if you can, near an orange emergency phone. Switch on your hazard warning lights.

Note: there's an emergency phone about every mile – the arrows on the posts at the back of the hard shoulder point you in the direction of the nearest one.

- Use the *left-hand door* to get out of the vehicle; make sure your passengers do too.
- Keep everyone *away from the carriageway* – up on the bank if possible.
- Animals should stay in the vehicle, unless you are sure they would not be safe there.
- When you make your call on the emergency phone (which is free), give full details of your vehicle and location to the police; tell them if you feel especially at risk for any reason. Then go back and wait in a safe place near the vehicle.

Never under-estimate how dangerous the hard shoulder can be. As many as one in eight road deaths happen there.

TEST YOUR UNDERSTANDING OF THIS SECTION

1. How can learner drivers get experience of motorway driving?

2. What should you always do before starting out on a long motorway journey?

3. What is the procedure for joining a motorway from a slip road?

4. How would you deal with the situation if a suitcase were to fall from your roof rack on to the motorway?

5. In what circumstances could you 'overtake on the left' on a motorway?

6. What does an overhead light signal with a red cross mean?

7. When you leave the motorway, what kind of road sign can you expect to see next?

8. How should you proceed when you see a 'lane closure' sign?

9. Where would you find green reflective studs used on a motorway?

10. For what reason are you allowed to stop on the hard shoulder?

Answers on page 192–3

Other road users

How am I driving?

The number of vehicles on the road in 1998 was 27.5 million; almost twice as many as 30 years ago.

You may encounter drivers making unexpected errors at the departure points for airports and ferry ports. This isn't surprising if they have just arrived from a country where they drive on the right.

As we said earlier, a car is not an offensive weapon; but sadly, it has the potential to become one.

When you go out driving, do you feel:

- as if you're going into a battlefield – threatened by other drivers and in competition with them?

or

- as if you're part of what an early film about the Driving Test called 'The Fellowship of the Road'?

Perhaps a modern-day parallel for that sense of camaraderie might be found among truck drivers – people with a common interest in skilled driving (see 'Motorists with attitude', page 46). You'll notice how they try to cooperate on the road, and many work for companies who have enrolled their staff in schemes such as 'How's My Driving?' which prioritise road safety. But just how far has this sense of mutual responsibility extended to **car drivers**?

Our roads are becoming more crowded all the time; driving in today's heavy traffic demands quite a high level of skill, and you don't have much room for error.

Today's driving demands a lot of patience and consideration.

As drivers we need to cooperate with each other on the road, to keep the traffic flowing smoothly and ensure road safety.

If you're a learner driver, you hope that others will make allowances for your inexperience.

If you're an experienced driver, you can remember what it was like to be a learner, and anticipate that they're sometimes going to stall, or that they may not 'make normal progress'.

So *consideration* is the key word; here are some suggestions that apply to general driving.

- *Don't assume you have priority;* and even when you know you do, be prepared to *give way* if you can see that this is the best way to prevent an accident.
- Always give **clear signals**: in good time, where possible; and *cancel* the signal when you've finished moving in that direction. (As a driver, you need to know all the arm signals shown in *The Highway Code*, to that you can understand the meaning of any arm signals used by another road user, such as a cyclist or horserider, even if you are unlikely to need to use them yourself.)
- When turning right, move into position *in plenty of time* so that other drivers know what you're doing.
- Obey any signals from:
  police officers
  traffic wardens
  school crossing patrols.

- Where possible, make 'normal progress'.
- Drive at the right speed for the road you're on, *keeping* to speed limits and *adjusting your speed downwards* for bad weather, road-works etc.
- *Anticipate* bends, junctions and roundabouts by slowing down in advance. Be ready to change gear.
- Don't weave in and out of **traffic queues**, or make use of 'rat-runs' to try and gain a few extra feet.
- *Be aware* of more vulnerable road users (see 'Road users at risk', page 132).
- And finally – remember that *anyone can make a mistake*, or have an off-day!

To sum up: a sense of shared responsibility *can* be cool – and it can even be good for your insurance premiums!

If a police-car patrol wants you to stop for any reason, they will use their flashing blue lights and left indicators. You must pull over and stop (having checked that it's safe by using MSM); when you stop, *switch off your engine.*

TEST YOUR UNDERSTANDING
OF THIS SECTION

1. Why should you be on the look-out for hazards around airports and ferry ports?

2. The indicators on modern cars are very efficient, so why do you still need to learn about arm signals before taking your test?

3. If a police car is following you, how will the police let you know if they want you to stop?

4. What sort of problems are caused by 'rat-runs'?

5. How should you approach a bend in the road?

Answers on page 194

I'm right behind you!

Drivers closing on you at high speed with headlights blazing, horns blaring and fingers raised in unmistakable gestures – any new driver who's experienced this kind of harassment knows how frightening it can be.

You assume you must have done something wrong, or that the driver behind can see a problem with your car and is trying to draw your attention to it. Unfortunately, in the vast majority of cases it's neither of these; you have simply incurred the wrath of an impatient driver who's letting you know in no uncertain terms that he (or she) wants you to *get out of the way!*

Even if you're confident that you're in the right place on the road – and driving at the correct speed for the type of road and conditions – the best response is to allow the driver behind to pass you.

Remember the *two-second rule!* If you slow down to give more room between your car and the one in front, you're protecting both yourself *and* the driver behind.

Sometimes glare is due to badly adjusted headlights – or even bumps in the road which make it look as though another car is flashing you.

When your car is unusually heavily loaded, you may need to make an adjustment to the angle of the headlights.

TAILGATING

Driving excessively close up behind another vehicle is known as tailgating – and it's dangerous!

The car in front may stop suddenly (e.g. to avoid hitting a child or animal that has dashed out into the road); the car following runs the risk of crashing into it (especially if the brakes are faulty).

Rear-end shunts account for a large percentage of all accidents (see 'Motorists with attitude', page 46). In these situations, the driver of the car behind is almost always judged to be the guilty party.

So tailgating can be expensive as well as dangerous.

Another time when drivers are tempted to tailgate is when attempting to pass a large slow-moving vehicle.

However, *keeping well back* improves your view of the road ahead, so that you're better able to judge when it's safe to overtake.

LIGHT-SENSITIVE

In Part 2 we mentioned the habit of some drivers of using headlights and fog lights to intimidate others (see 'Lighting up the night', page 100).

The Highway Code warns against using lights in any way that could cause discomfort to other drivers. This includes:

- flashing your headlights as you come up behind another car to signal them to get out of the way
- flashing at an approaching motorist in such a way as to dazzle them – this could cause them to lose control temporarily
- using full beam headlights when you should revert to dipped – this can reflect in the rear view mirror of the car in front, making it impossible for the driver to see clearly.

If you are being dazzled by headlights, don't be intimidated, but slow down or stop until you can see to proceed safely. You can also dip your rear-view mirror. See also 'Fog lights' on page 100 – these rules also apply to driving with fog lights in daylight.

How do I warn other drivers of a hazard ahead?

The Highway Code tells you not to flash other motorists to warn them of a hazard, although it has to be said, this is what many drivers in fact do.

The rule says that you should only flash your lights to let others know you're there.

But it *is* permissible to use your **hazard warning lights**, as follows:

- if your vehicle has broken down and is causing a traffic obstruction
- if you are driving on a motorway or national speed limit dual carriageway and you need to warn other drivers that there's a hazard ahead. But only switch them on for a short time, until you judge that the danger has passed.

Except in the situation described above –

never drive with your hazard warning lights on.

SOUND THAT HORN

Compared with the conventions in some other countries, there are very few occasions when you can use your horn.

It's often wrongly used:

as a form of greeting when you're driving along and see someone you know; or by harassed parents providing a 'taxi service' who want their children to know they've arrived to transport them to their next destination.

But it should be used:

only to let other drivers know you're there (just like the lights, above). Places where you would sound your horn include when you're coming up to a hump-back bridge or a completely blind corner.

In addition, don't sound your horn:

- at horses
- in a built-up area between 11.30pm and 7.00am
- when you're sitting in your car while it's stationary – unless you can see another vehicle heading towards you in a dangerous manner and need to attract the driver's attention.

The horn is an **audible warning signal** and should be kept for dangerous situations only.

At a motorway hazard, allow long enough for two or three cars to build up behind, then switch your hazard warning lights off.

Don't rely on using your horn to make pedestrians get out of your way – what if the pedestrian happens to be deaf? It's the motorist's responsibility to look out for hazards and give pedestrians plenty of room.

TEST YOUR UNDERSTANDING
OF THIS SECTION

1. What is meant by tailgating, and why should you avoid doing it?

2. Why could flashing your headlights be a danger to other drivers?

3. When are you allowed to switch on your hazard warning lights?

4. In what situations should you sound your horn?

5. Is it always wrong to sound your horn when the car is stationary?

Answers on page 195

It's not me, it's the others!

This is a fair point!

It's very annoying to find that, when you've been following some rule of the road to the letter, another driver proceeds to take advantage of your care and consideration.

But in today's demanding driving conditions

YOU NEED TO THINK FOR OTHER DRIVERS AS WELL AS YOURSELF.

Here are some potentially hazardous situations where you could find yourself feeling resentful because of the actions of **other drivers**.

DRIVING AT THE CORRECT SPEED LIMIT

If you're doing 30mph and that's the correct speed limit for the road you're on, what is your reaction going to be if another driver comes up fast behind you, flashing their lights and maybe sounding the horn?

You might react by:

- speeding up to get away from him/her
- deliberately slowing down to annoy the other driver
- adjusting your position on the road so that the car behind can't overtake.

However, the best thing to do is to *let them overtake*, so that you can get on with driving at the appropriate speed in peace.

Remember that the vehicle behind is the one in the wrong in this situation (see 'Tailgating', page 118).

Don't forget the two-second rule. Change it to four seconds in wet weather, and 20 seconds when there's ice on the roads.

Although you sometimes need to think for other drivers, it's not safe to make decisions for them about when they should overtake.

BEING 'CUT UP' BY OTHER DRIVERS

If you drive regularly, especially on country roads, you'll be aware that some drivers take astonishing risks when overtaking; on hills, approaching bends, and in many other places where they cannot possibly see the road ahead far enough to overtake safely.

An example of this is where a dual carriageway is about to end and vehicles are speeding along the outside lane to get as far as possible before the road reverts to a single lane.

It's quite understandable that you might feel tempted to:
- accelerate to get up close behind them
- flash your headlights
- sound the horn for a long time.

But again, the best thing is to *let them get on with it* – and improve your own position by *dropping back so that you can keep the correct separation gap* between you and the car in front (see 'Stopping distances', page 84).

DRIVING A SLOW VEHICLE

When you're driving a slow-moving vehicle, especially if it's on a narrow road, or a road with a series of bends, you may become the target for frustration from drivers behind who want to get past.

You might think:
- the safest thing you can do is steer closer to the centre of the road and prevent the cars behind from overtaking, since they won't be able to do so safely
- that it's up to you to wave them on when you can see it's safe for them to overtake
- that you shouldn't wave them on, you should use your left indicator to tell them to go past.

The correct action is to *pull in when you find a safe place* and let the traffic which has built up behind you go past.

SAFETY MARGINS AND YOUR DRIVING TEST

During your test, your ability to judge safety margins accurately will be observed throughout the route.

Concentrate on getting used to *judging distances*. How far away is:

- the car behind?
- the car in front?
- the car coming towards you?

Do you have room to overtake safely?

- Before you overtake, use the MSM routine. It's slightly different for overtaking. Use your mirror to check for following vehicles, then position yourself slightly further out than normal to get a view past the vehicle in front. Signal (the driver can see your signal in his or her mirror), then check your mirrors again before moving out to overtake.

- *Don't overtake* if you would have to exceed the speed limit to get past the other car.
- *Give way* if there is an obstruction such as a parked car on your side of the road. (See 'Who goes first?', page 125.) *Be prepared to give way* even if the obstruction is on the **opposite** side of the road.
- *Allow plenty of room* (see the diagram below) – cyclists and motorcyclists need to be given at least as much room as the width of a car, since they could swerve, and horses even more room in case they bolt.
- Lastly – when you have decided it's safe to overtake, then *be positive about it*; try not to lose your nerve half-way!

But, like all other driving skills, overtaking improves with regular practice as your ability to judge distances improves.

If you are driving past parked cars, it's a good idea to leave as much space as the width of a car door – in case one opens suddenly. If you can't give that much space, slow down so that you could stop if necessary.

TEST YOUR UNDERSTANDING OF THIS SECTION

1. Is it against the law to flash your headlights at a car that has cut in front of you after overtaking?

2. What is the correct way for the driver of a heavy lorry to signal to you that it is safe to overtake?

3. How should you change the 'two-second rule' when driving in bad weather?

4. How much room should you allow when overtaking a motorcyclist?

5. Once you have started to overtake another vehicle, what should you do next?

Answers on page 196

Who goes first?

A simple way to think about who has priority on the road is that the more powerful gives way to the less powerful.

Or, if you've got four wheels you give way to someone who has two, or none at all (i.e. travelling on foot, or on a horse or other beast of burden).

The point here is that just because another type of road user is slower than the majority (cars), it doesn't mean that they don't have priority.

BUT –

of course it's also necessary to give way to other wheeled vehicles when they are large or difficult to manoeuvre: this includes buses, long vehicles, tractors, trams and many more.

Listed on the next pages are some categories of road user that have priority over cars.

Note: this information applies to *non-motorway* roads; vehicles not suited to the higher speeds of motorway traffic are *not allowed on the motorway*. These include motorcycles under 50cc, cyclists, horses, agricultural vehicles and invalid carriages.

Remember: part of learning to drive safely is being able to control the car at very slow speeds, as when following a cyclist (see 'Can you handle it?', page 18).

PEDESTRIANS

(See also 'Pedestrian crossings', pages 74–5.)

Pedestrians have priority:

- when they have started to cross a road that you want to turn into, *even if there isn't a pedestrian crossing there*
- when they have started to cross on a pelican crossing, *even if the flashing light comes on before they reach the far side*
- when they have stepped on to a zebra crossing. You don't *have* to stop for pedestrians who are standing on the pavement by the beacon but who haven't actually set foot on the crossing; but it's generally accepted that drivers *should* give way to pedestrians waiting to cross. When you're taking your **driving test**, your examiner will expect you to stop if there are any pedestrians approaching the zebra crossing who may wish to cross. Show extra consideration to children, elderly people and people with disabilities at pedestrian crossings.

BUSES AND TRAMS

Bus drivers have to rely on motorists giving way to let them pull out after they've stopped to pick up and drop off passengers. So, when you see a bus signalling to pull out, check that it's safe (using MSM) and then slow down and *give way* to the bus.

You should always give way to **trams**, because they cannot steer to avoid you (see the list of hazards in 'I didn't even see him…', page 52). Don't try to overtake them – especially between the tram tracks and the left-hand kerb, if the trams run in the centre of the road. Take extra care because *trams are sometimes allowed to proceed when you are not* – usually there are traffic signals just for them.

CYCLISTS

It's all too easy for cyclists to become 'invisible' to motorists when driving in busy town traffic; so, try to be aware of cyclists and give way to them.

Cyclists have priority in **cycle lanes** (see 'Other types of lanes', page 73).

They have priority when riding across **toucan crossings** (see page 75) when the lights are in their favour.

You should also *give way* to cyclists crossing in front of you when approaching roundabouts and junctions; and *stay well back* even when they have not yet crossed to the correct lane, since a cyclist intending to turn right may well signal their intention while still in the left lane (see page 71).

HORSES AND LIVESTOCK

When driving past **horse riders**, give them plenty of room; they have priority over cars.

Horse riders, in turn, have responsibilities towards other road users. They must:
- keep to the left
- never ride more than two abreast
- ride in single file when on a narrow road, or approaching a bend.

When driving on country roads there's always a chance of meeting a herd of **sheep** or **cows** (see page 170), so be prepared for this.

As with horses –
- give them plenty of room
- don't sound your horn at them
- stop and switch off your engine until they have moved on.

Note: a person in charge of a herd of animals may approach you and ask you to stop while they get them across the road; even though this isn't an 'authorised person' such as a police officer, it's still right to comply with their request.

People riding horses on the road are often children, so you need to take extra care; when you see two riders abreast, it may well be that the one on the outside is shielding a less experienced rider.

When following a long vehicle, take a look at the markers on the sides and end. They are there to warn you of the length of the vehicle, and sometimes of overhanging loads.

LARGE VEHICLES

A large vehicle approaching a junction or roundabout may take up a position on the road that would be wrong for a car (see 'Lanes and roundabouts', page 71).

They may keep to the left lane while intending to turn right – or the other way round.

They do this because they need extra road space to carry out their manoeuvre, due to their length.

Long vehicles turning into minor roads

A long vehicle that needs to turn left off a major road into a minor road may prepare to do so by moving out towards the centre of the road, or even moving across to the other side.

If you're following them:

- *give way*, and don't try to overtake – on the right *or* the left
- you might need to slow down and *stop* while the driver of the long vehicle makes the turn.

If you're the one on the minor road, waiting to turn on to a major road:

- don't risk pulling out while the long vehicle is approaching, even if you're turning left and think you've got plenty of time to get out ahead of them
- be aware: there might be a driver speeding along the main road and overtaking the long vehicle; while overtaking they will be hidden from your view. (This can apply to *any* vehicle that masks another – not just to long vehicles.)
- because the long vehicle needs space to manoeuvre when straightening out of its turn, be prepared to clear the junction, or stay well back from it to give the long vehicle more room.

VEHICLES WITH FLASHING COLOURED BEACONS

As a general rule, give way to vehicles with flashing beacons.

Blue beacons are used by:

- ambulances
- fire engines
- police
- other emergency vehicles.

As well as beacon lights, these vehicles use flashing headlights or sirens, or both, to alert other drivers.

Green beacons are used by doctors attending emergency calls.

The way to react when you see a vehicle with a blue or green flashing beacon coming up behind you is to

GET OUT OF THE WAY!

You have to take care not to cause another accident by your actions, so use your mirrors to anticipate where the emergency vehicle is trying to go, then do your best to make it easier for them to get through. If possible, pull over to the side of the road to let them pass.

Orange beacons are used by:

- accident recovery vehicles
- breakdown vehicles
- gritting lorries and other slow vehicles
- motorway maintenance vehicles
- vehicles with unusually heavy or awkward loads
- slow vehicles driven by people with disabilities (max speed 8mph).

Although these are not emergency vehicles, you may need to slow down and give them priority, as they are difficult to manoeuvre.

The flashing orange beacon alerts you to a **hazard**.

Other vehicles that display blue flashing beacons include:

- **blood transfusion units**
- **bomb disposal teams**
- **coastguards**
- **mountain rescue teams.**

Where there's more than one mini-roundabout at a crossroads or junction, treat each one separately and give way to the right.

GIVING WAY IN NORMAL DRIVING

- At a **junction with a broken white line** across the road, traffic on the major road has priority (see 'Crossing the line', page 79).
- Traffic **on a motorway** has priority over traffic joining from a slip road (see 'Motorway rules', page 107).
- At **roundabouts**, traffic coming **from the right** has priority (see 'Lanes and roundabouts', page 71).
- Where there isn't enough room for two vehicles to pass, due to an **obstruction** such as parked cars, the driver whose side the obstruction is on should give way.
- When driving on **single-track roads** where two vehicles cannot pass side by side, make use of the proper passing places. Don't drive so fast that you can't stop if you meet someone coming the other way; reverse into a passing place if necessary, or stop immediately before one on the opposite side so that the other driver can pass.

(For more tips on country driving, see page 170.)

- This sign means **oncoming traffic** has priority over you.

But use caution even if you have priority, as not everyone understands the different signs.

- When **traffic lights are out of order** (see 'Crossroads with traffic lights', page 66) the junction becomes like an unmarked crossroads, so no one has priority. Often drivers will show more care than usual, because they *know* this is a hazardous situation.

Note: some drivers observe their own rules about who has priority – rules that don't figure in *The Highway Code!*

One of these is when male drivers believe they always have priority over female drivers, and expect to go first at junctions (and sometimes it's the other way around)! They get very annoyed if a female driver overtakes them, and hold the view that women are not safe to be on the road.

There is of course no logical reason for this belief, since statistics show that women are safer drivers.

TEST YOUR UNDERSTANDING OF THIS SECTION

1. If a car driver is using their indicators to show that they intend to turn into a side road, and there is an elderly pedestrian on the pavement waiting to cross, who has priority – the car or the pedestrian?

2. What should you bear in mind when driving on a road where trams operate?

3. When must you give way to cyclists?

4. Why do you sometimes see horse riders two abreast?

5. Are you required to stop if asked to do so by a person herding animals?

6. How should you react if a long vehicle pulls out towards the *centre* of the road in front of you when they are signalling to turn *left*?

7. Why would it not be safe to pull out of a side road if you can see that the vehicle to your left on the main road is intending to turn into the side road?

8. How should you adjust your normal driving when an ambulance with a flashing blue beacon appears behind you?

9. What is the correct procedure at double mini-roundabouts?

10. What sort of sign means 'oncoming traffic has priority'?

Answers on page 197

Road users at risk

In some countries cycle helmets are compulsory, and have been shown to reduce casualties, especially among the young.

We've already seen that there are several groups who are more at risk when out on the road than the drivers of cars and other vehicles.

They include:

- cyclists
- motorcyclists
- pedestrians
- horse riders
- learner drivers
- drivers who have recently passed their test
- people with disabilities.

Many road users who are not driving cars have nothing to protect them from the effects of an accident involving a car or any larger vehicle.

Cyclists and people riding motorcycles are more at risk than car drivers because:

- they are affected more by strong winds, or turbulence caused by other vehicles
- they are sometimes difficult for car drivers to see.

PEDESTRIANS MOST AT RISK

Children haven't yet developed a sense of danger on the road, and can't judge how close an approaching car is, or its speed.

They may:

- run out into the road without looking
- appear without warning from between parked vehicles (see 'I didn't even see him…', page 52)
- step into the road behind you while you're reversing – you may not see them behind you because of their size.

People who are unable to see and/or hear

A blind person will usually carry a **white stick** to alert you to their presence.

If the stick has a **red band**, this means that the person is also deaf, so will have no warning of an approaching car either visually or from engine noise.

Elderly people and others who have difficulty in walking

Some pedestrians need more time to walk across a pedestrian crossing, or to finish crossing a road you are waiting to turn into.

Don't hurry them or sound your horn, but wait until they have reached the pavement on the opposite side of the road before you drive on (see 'Who goes first?', page 126).

SIGNS THAT ALERT YOU TO ROAD USERS AT RISK

Advance warning of school crossing patrol.

School crossing patrol.

Pedestrians walking in the road ahead (no pavement).

Elderly or disabled people crossing.

Cycle lane and pedestrian route.

Sign on back of school bus or coach.

WALKERS IN AN ORGANISED GROUP

You may have to deal with a large group of people walking together – members of a ramblers' club, or perhaps young people out on a sponsored walk.

There are strict rules in *The Highway Code* that the walkers must follow:

- they should walk on the path if there is one, or otherwise keep to the *left*
- a 'look-out' should walk at each end of the line (carrying a light at night – **white** for the person at the front of the line, **red** at the rear)
- they should be wearing **fluorescent clothing** (reflective at night).

Provided they're doing all that, you should be able to see them in good time; and drive past them slowly and carefully when it's safe to do so, giving them plenty of room.

LEARNER DRIVERS

Some groups of motorists are known to be more at risk of accidents, especially young and inexperienced drivers (see 'Motorists with attitude', page 47).

They may not be so fast at reacting to hazards, and may sometimes make wrong judgements.

It's easy to spot a learner driver by the 'L' plate; but recently qualified drivers can also choose to display a 'P' plate (for 'Probationer') or a 'New Driver' plate.

DRIVERS WITH DISABILITIES

You can recognise a car driven by someone who's disabled because they display a **Blue Card** (formerly an Orange Badge).

This gives them the right to park in a space reserved for drivers with disabilities (see 'Where to park – and where not to', page 92).

The Blue Card also acts as a parking permit for disabled people visiting other countries in the European Union; they leave it open on display in the car and are then allowed the same rights as nationals in the country they're visiting.

Often disabled people drive cars that have been specially adapted for them, but you may also see small powered vehicles with a maximum speed of 8mph (see 'Orange flashing beacons', page 129). The orange beacon warns you that there is an unusually slow vehicle on the road.

In Northern Ireland, all new drivers must display 'R' plates for 12 months after passing their test, and may not drive faster than 45mph on any road during this time.

OTHER DRIVERS AT RISK

How much are you, as a driver, at risk on the road?

In general –

you're far safer **inside** a car than the more vulnerable road users **outside!**

Modern cars are built to extremely high standards of safety, and will withstand impacts more effectively than older models.

For example, SIPS stands for Side Impact Protection System; this means the car is designed to protect you as much as possible in the event of a sideways collision.

This may seem like good news, but in fact

IT'S A WORRY!

Safety experts have identified these improved safety features as a reason for complacency among young drivers, leading to them being less afraid of being badly injured in an accident, and therefore less cautious.

The **losers** in this are the pedestrians, cyclists and motorcyclists, who are far more likely to sustain serious injury in an accident involving a car travelling at *too high a speed* (see 'Motorists with attitude', page 49).

You can help by being aware that:

- if you hit a pedestrian when driving at **40mph**, the pedestrian will *probably be killed.*
- if you hit a pedestrian at **20mph**, the pedestrian *could* be killed or injured but stands a *far better chance of surviving* than at 40mph.

This is the thinking behind plans for the introduction of more 20mph speed limits in residential areas. Along with speed humps and other traffic-calming devices, the aim is to reduce accidents in streets where children regularly play, as well as around the entrances to schools.

You might think that 30mph is a safe speed, but statistics show that 50% of pedestrians hit by a car travelling at 30mph will be killed.

TEST YOUR UNDERSTANDING
OF THIS SECTION

1. Why are cyclists and motorcycle riders described as vulnerable road users?

2. Where should you especially watch out for children in the road?

3. Which sign gives you advance warning of a school crossing patrol?

4. In what way could the improved safety features of new cars pose a risk to other road users?

5. What is likely to happen if you hit a pedestrian while driving at 40mph?

Answers on page 198

Shift that load!

Once you've passed your driving test you'll be entitled to tow a small trailer, or a caravan, behind your car. (To tow larger caravans and trailers, you'll need to take another test.)

Driving with a load on tow involves:

- being able to call on reasonably advanced driving skills

- distributing the trailer's load correctly
- knowing, and keeping to, the restrictions on how much your vehicle can tow (see 'Towing', pages 86–7).

You might need to inflate your tyres to more than the normal pressure when towing a heavy load. Remember to change back to normal tyre pressure for your car when you complete your journey. Check your vehicle's handbook for advice on this.

DRIVING SKILLS NEEDED WHEN TOWING

Towing will affect the way your vehicle handles.

The extra *length* will affect:
- the road space you need to have in order to overtake
- the road position you'll need to take up before making a turn at a roundabout or junction (see 'Large vehicles', page 128).

The extra *weight* will affect:
- how long it takes you to accelerate and pull away
- how much work the engine has to do
- how long it takes you to brake and stop (see 'Stopping distances', page 84).

SO – THINK ABOUT WHAT YOUR STOPPING DISTANCE NEEDS TO BE WITH THE EXTRA WEIGHT.

Common sense tells you to drive more slowly when you're towing, but check *The Highway Code* for the official speed limits – they're generally 10mph lower on *all* major roads and dual carriageways, not just on motorways.

DRIVING WITH A ROOF RACK

If you've got a roof rack or cycle rack as well as a caravan or trailer it will make an additional difference to the way your vehicle handles; the extra weight has to be deducted from the total MAM (see page 86).

Be aware that a loaded roofrack can add considerable height to your vehicle.

SNAKING

You may have had the experience of driving along a road gasping in disbelief as the caravan in front lurches wildly from side to side behind the car that's pulling it.

So that you don't end up with similar problems, *check:*

- that the load is properly distributed
- that the tow bar is securely attached
- that the coupling height is correct.

What to do about snaking

If you do have to deal with a trailer that starts to snake (weaves from side to side) it means you are probably driving too fast, so lower your overall speed –

- ease off the accelerator, and don't brake
- regain control of the steering
- apply the brakes gently.

Horseboxes

Don't be tempted to drive too fast when you are towing a horsebox. If it starts to snake, use the same technique to regain control.

DISTRIBUTING THE LOAD

If the weight of the load is arranged properly, this should cut down the risk of *snaking, swerving* and *losing control.*

Loading a trailer

Load the goods into the trailer with the weight distributed **as evenly as possible** – avoid loading more weight towards the front, or the rear, or to one side.

Loading a caravan – Goods

The technique here is to load any heavy items for the trip

- as low as possible inside the caravan
- mainly over the axles
- safely secured so that they don't roll around.

Loading a caravan – People

There isn't any room for argument here – passengers can't travel in a vehicle that's being towed.

A stabiliser attached to the towbar can help in making your tow load/trailer more secure.

Towing a trailer may mean you need to amend your car's insurance cover. Always get advice to make sure that the combination you're driving meets current EU regulations.

Tyres are available that are specially designed for trailers. It may not be easy to find a replacement in an emergency, so carry a spare.

PROJECTING LOADS

(See 'Towing', page 86.)

It's against the law to have a load on tow that's sticking out in a dangerous manner (see your copy of *The Highway Code*).

LOADS NOT TIED DOWN SECURELY

The same legal necessity applies here; you *must* make your load secure, so that it doesn't pose a danger to other road users.

If the worst happens and something falls from your trailer while you're on the motorway, or a suitcase falls from your roof rack, remember the correct procedure (see 'Motorway do's and don'ts', page 108).

Remember that where there are three or more lanes on a motorway, the outside lane is not available for use by vehicles towing trailers (see page 108). Any vehicle that's towing a caravan or trailer must return to the left lane as soon as possible after overtaking.

PARKING WITH A TRAILER

Take extra care when choosing where to park with a trailer, so that you don't obstruct gates or driveways (see page 92).

Remember – if you park at night with a trailer attached, it must have lights (see page 86).

In the next section we'll look at what you can and can't do when carrying **passengers** in your car.

TEST YOUR UNDERSTANDING OF THIS SECTION

1. What difference does towing a caravan or trailer make to the way your car handles?

2. When and why could snaking occur?

3. How should goods be loaded into a trailer?

4. Can you use your caravan to take additional people with you on holiday if there is not enough room for them in the car?

5. What should you bear in mind when parking a car that has a trailer attached?

Answers on page 199

It's your responsibility

Most other countries operate similar rules about child restraints and seat belt wearing. Some countries do not allow children to travel in the front seat below a certain age.

You're responsible for the safety of any passengers who travel in your car.

This is especially important when your passengers include **children**.

Try to make it clear that when children are travelling in your car, you expect them to sit still and not to distract you, the driver (see 'Concentration', page 56).

The Highway Code makes it quite clear that it's down to **you** to see that any children travelling in your car are 'restrained' as required by law.

Note: a 'child' in this instance is someone under 14.

APPROPRIATE RESTRAINTS

Children under 3

- a child seat, or booster seat (the right one for the child's weight)
- a harness
- a baby seat, or baby carrier.

Don't's

Small children *shouldn't* be strapped in using an *adult seat belt*, which could cause them injury and wouldn't be guaranteed to keep them safely seated.

A *lap belt* also should not be used by a child.

Nor should you allow an adult to sit holding the child on their knee.

Children aged 3–11 and under 1.5m (5 feet) tall

- should be strapped in using an appropriate child restraint if possible; failing that, an adult seat belt is allowed.

Children aged 12–13 (or younger, if taller than 1.5m)

- adult seat belts should be worn.

(See also 'Seat belts', page 39.)

CHILD LOCKS

These are provided so that the driver can prevent child passengers from accidentally opening the **rear doors**.

(Opinions are divided about whether you should lock *all* doors while driving; one view is that it's an unsafe habit to get into, since it would make it more difficult to get passengers out in an accident if all the car's doors were locked. An alternative view is that locking all doors keeps the occupants safe from unwanted outside interference, e.g. when stationary at traffic lights. Central locking gives you the option of locking all doors temporarily in potentially threatening situations, then releasing them again.)

CARRYING CHILDREN IN ESTATE CARS/HATCHBACKS

You may sometimes have seen one or more children sitting in the back section of a hatchback, i.e. behind the rear seats, while the vehicle is in motion.

This is another *DON'T!*

Children travelling in this way have no seat belts, and so could be thrown forward if you had to stop suddenly in an emergency – they could injure themselves and other passengers.

REAR-FACING BABY SEATS

DON'T fit one of these into a *front seat protected by an airbag*.

If the airbag inflated the baby could be thrown violently against the seat back.

Adult passengers have responsibility for themselves in law, but it makes sense to remind them if you can see they haven't fastened their seat belts. In an accident, passengers in the back who aren't wearing their seat belts could be thrown forward, crushing those in the front seats.

TEST YOUR UNDERSTANDING OF THIS SECTION

1. If a child and his or her parent are travelling in your car, is the parent responsible for the child's safety?

2. What is an appropriate restraint for a child aged under 3 travelling in your car?

3. If you don't have child restraints in your car, can the child use an adult seat belt instead?

4. Why should children not travel in the space behind the rear seat of a hatchback?

5. What should you bear in mind when positioning a rear-facing baby seat?

Answers on page 200

Trust me, I'm a First-Aider

Would you be able to help someone injured in a road accident?

Some people fight shy of giving assistance, on the basis that 'a little knowledge is a dangerous thing', so they might do more harm than good.

BUT –

if you can get some basic training and become more confident about being able to give the right kind of First Aid, then it's good news for you and for the accident victim –

● because you'll be better able to cope in the most hazardous

situations you'll encounter, making you generally a safer driver.

This section covers First Aid and road accident procedure, gives a summary of what you need to carry in your car, and explains what to do about reporting an accident in which you are involved.

Study the information on accidents and First Aid in your copy of *The Highway Code* very carefully – it's so important that it gets two separate sections.

You can learn the right way to give First Aid from classes run by the St John and St Andrew's Ambulance Associations, or from the British Red Cross – find their numbers in your local phone directory. It's not difficult and it could save a life.

Sterile dressings come in sealed packages. If the seal is damaged or broken, it is no longer safe, and you need to replace the whole dressing.

YOUR FIRST AID KIT

First Aid kits are available from garages and motor accessory stores, and come with their contents already assembled. Either invest in one of these, or make up your own kit, which could include:

- plasters (non-allergenic are safest)
- bandages
- safety-pins
- scissors

- a range of sterile dressings (for burns and other injuries)
- antiseptic wipes (for minor cuts and grazes)
- disposable gloves.

Keep your First Aid kit handy in the car, so you can find it quickly if you need to.

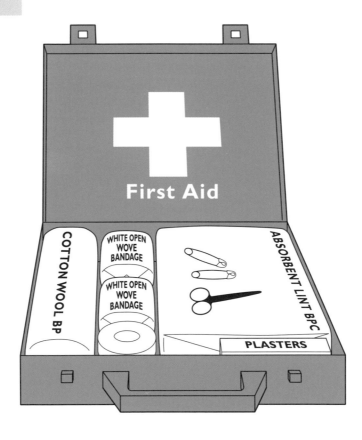

OTHER EMERGENCY ITEMS

Some other useful items *to keep in the car* in case of emergency are:

- sunglasses
- warning triangle
- fire extinguisher
- torch
- blanket
- emergency supplies of food/drink (see 'Driving in snow', page 103).

Other items to carry with you on all journeys *but **not necessarily** leave in the car* include:

- insurance certificate
- driving licence
- Vehicle Registration Document (when driving abroad)
- phone card and/or credit card
- motoring organisation membership card
- spare keys

- spare bulbs and fuses
- car manual
- tow rope
- jump leads
- rag (non-oily)
- container of water (to drink if you break down and have to wait, or to top up a leaking radiator)
- de-icer and scraper (winter)
- sunglasses (summer or winter – snow can be dazzling).

There are different priorities if the accident involves a vehicle carrying dangerous goods. See your copy of *The Highway Code* for more information.

ACCIDENT AHEAD!

Your first warning of an accident on the road ahead will probably be the sound of emergency vehicles, or seeing flashing beacons coming up behind (see 'Vehicles with flashing coloured beacons', page 129).

Slow down and be prepared to **stop** if necessary.

But *don't do so only for the purpose of getting a better look at the accident!* – for example, when you see an accident on the opposite side of a motorway or dual carriageway.

Otherwise, stop if you can give assistance, switching on your hazard warning lights (see 'Light-sensitive', page 118).

ACCIDENT PROCEDURE

At the scene of an accident it is important to **assess** the situation first and **check for any danger**. Try to keep a clear head. You must not become a casualty yourself:

- check that no one is smoking
- check that all vehicle engines have been *switched off*
- make sure anyone who isn't injured moves *well away* from the traffic (on a motorway, away from the hard shoulder and central reservation onto the embankment)
- *call the emergency services* on 999 if this hasn't been done already, giving full details of location and how many vehicles involved (on a **motorway**, use the emergency roadside phone – see 'Motorway rules', page 111)
- don't move anyone who is seriously injured – unless there is a risk of fire or explosion
- **give First Aid** to anyone injured
- **stay** till the emergency services arrive.

FIRST AID

If you are first on the scene and people have been hurt, it can be difficult to know where to start. It helps to remember the **'ABC'** of First Aid:

A is for Airway

B is for Breathing

C is for Circulation

This tells you what to attend to first when you look at any casualty.

Airway

If an injured person is breathing but unconscious, place them in the recovery position illustrated on page 145 and monitor them carefully for ABC.

If an injured person is not breathing, first make sure nothing is blocking the back of their throat – check for obstructions in the mouth.

Breathing

If clearing the airway has not resulted in the person starting to breathe:

- lift the chin
- tilt the head backwards carefully to open the airway

- pinch the nostrils and blow into the mouth until the chest rises
- repeat this every four seconds until the person can breathe unaided, or help arrives.

Circulation

This means bleeding. If a person is bleeding, apply firm pressure to the wound for up to 10 minutes, until the bleeding slows or stops. You can then cover it with a sterile dressing. An injured limb can be raised to lessen bleeding – as long as it isn't broken.

In addition to using the **'ABC'**, you can help by speaking in a reassuring way to the injured person, who is likely to be in shock.

You can try to make them more comfortable and provide a blanket or coat to keep them warm, but avoid moving them unnecessarily, and *DON'T* give them anything to drink.

Forget about hot sweet tea and anything else that used to be recommended for shock! You must not give an injured person anything to eat or drink – it could delay vital hospital treatment which would require a general anaesthetic.

A question that comes up frequently is: *should you try to remove the helmet from an injured motorcyclist?*

The answer in almost every case is 'NO'.

If you are unfortunate enough to be involved in an accident yourself, here's what to do (provided you are not injured):

- **stop** your car. If you can't pull safely off the road, switch on hazard warning lights and place your warning triangle at least 45 metres (147 feet) behind your vehicle on the same side of the road. Take care not to place the triangle where it would cause a hazard.
  Note: never use warning triangles on motorways.
- observe the safety precautions given in 'Accident procedure' above.
- *stand in a safe place* – not between your car and oncoming traffic.

LEGAL REQUIREMENTS – DOCUMENTS

In any accident involving damage to property or to another vehicle, or injury to a person or animal, you must stop and provide the following information 'to anyone with reasonable grounds for requiring them':

- your name and address
- the name and address of the vehicle's owner, if it isn't you.

Do I have to tell the police?

If anyone has been injured in the accident, then it **must** be reported to the police.

If no police are at the scene, report the accident to them as soon as possible *(no longer than 24 hours after the accident)*; and take documents, including your insurance certificate, to the police station within seven days.

It's a good idea to make a record of the events:

- *write down* what happened (noting the time of the accident), sign and date it, and get signatures from other people present if you can – *make a note* of the details of the other drivers involved, and also any witnesses

- *draw a diagram* of the position of the vehicles on the road – or take a photograph, if you have a camera with you
- *record* all road markings and traffic signs at and around the scene
- *make a note of the weather conditions* at the time (e.g. wet road, fog).

This will come in useful later if you need to make an insurance claim.

What if no one was injured?

'Damage-only' accidents have to be reported to the police only if you were **not** able to give your name and address to any interested parties.

DEALING WITH OTHER PROBLEMS

Although less serious than accidents, there are other unexpected mishaps that can occur during driving, such as burst tyres and punctures.

Burst tyres

If a tyre bursts you will start to lose control of the car.

Don't brake suddenly, but pull up slowly when it's safe to do so, keeping a firm grip on the steering wheel. If you can't find a sufficiently safe place to change the tyre yourself, or if you're on a motorway, then call for breakdown assistance.

Punctures

The worst place to get a puncture is, of course, a motorway.

If you do get one:
- pull up on the hard shoulder
- use the emergency phone to call for assistance.

Lastly –
> don't ignore any **warning lights** that come on while you're driving. Prompt attention to the problem will minimise the risk of having an accident later.

The markers at the side of the motorway show the direction to the nearest phone.

TEST YOUR UNDERSTANDING OF THIS SECTION

1. What items should you carry in your car in case someone is injured in an accident?

2. Why is it important that no one smokes at the scene of an accident?

3. What details should you have ready when you call the emergency services?

4. Should your first priority be to pull injured people out of the road?

5. What is the 'ABC of First Aid'?

6. What should you give an injured person to drink?

7. What are the regulations concerning warning triangles?

8. At an accident scene, who is legally allowed to ask for your details?

9. After an accident, how long do you have before you must report it to the police?

10. If you get a puncture on the motorway, can you change the wheel on the hard shoulder?

Answers on page 201

Taking the test – and beyond

Applying for your test

**Check with
your driving
instructor what
the current
pass mark is
when you take
your test, as
the government
may change
it from time
to time.**

You have to pass two tests before you can apply for a full driving licence: the **Theory Test** and the **Practical Test**.

The Theory Test comes first, and you have to pass this before you can apply for the Practical Test.

You have to take the Practical Test within **two years** of passing the Theory Test.

You'll need your **Theory Test pass certificate** with you when you take your Practical Test.

WHAT IS THE THEORY TEST?

- There are 35 multiple-choice questions to be answered in 40 minutes.
- You answer them using a touch-screen.
- You have to get around 85% of them right to pass the test – currently 30 out of the 35 questions.

WHAT DOES THE THEORY TEST COVER?

All of the topics covered in this book can appear in your Theory Test.

The questions are devised by the **Driving Standards Agency (DSA)** and fall into the following categories:

- alertness
- attitude
- safety and your vehicle
- safety margins
- hazard awareness
- vulnerable road users
- other types of vehicle
- vehicle handling
- motorway rules
- rules of the road
- road and traffic signs
- documents
- accidents
- vehicle loading.

HOW IS THE THEORY TEST ORGANISED?

You can take your Theory Test at your local centre – there are over 150 in Great Britain and Northern Ireland. At some centres tests can be taken on Saturdays as well as weekdays, or during the evening.

Find out where your nearest centre is by asking your driving instructor – or you can call the **DSA information line** on 0870 01 01 372.

You should get an appointment within about two weeks (although it can take a little longer for drivers with special needs).

HOW CAN I PREPARE FOR THE THEORY TEST?

- Your instructor will have been talking to you about the Theory Test in the course of your driving lessons (see 'Who's in charge?', page 29).

He or she should be able to supply you with practice papers, or you can buy sets of sample questions from the DSA. Sample questions on CD Roms are also available for use on a computer.

- You should make sure you know your *Highway Code* inside out.
- It makes sense to invest in a **reliable book** of the *latest* official questions so that you can go through them and test your knowledge beforehand; *Driving Test Theory*, published by the AA, has all the questions and the diagrams and pictures that go with them, and the answers are at the back of the book so that you can test yourself.

If you can, try to stop yourself using a book to learn the questions and answers off by heart. For a start, there are now too many of them – almost a thousand! – and besides, the aim of the Theory Test is to increase your general understanding of *why* the rules about driving are the way they are.

You can pay for your Theory Test over the phone using a credit card, provided you're the cardholder. (Otherwise a cardholder can make the booking for you.) You'll need your provisional licence when you call. At the time of writing the cost is £15.50.

APPLYING FOR YOUR PRACTICAL TEST

You can book your test either by *filling in a form*, or *over the phone*. Make sure you book well in advance.

Application forms

You can get one of these from any DSA driving test centre – the number of the form is **DL26**.

You can also get one from your Approved Driving Instructor.

You can state the date on which you'd like to take the test.

At the time of writing the cost is £36.75, but this rises to £46 if you want to take your test during the evening or on a Saturday. (Evening appointments are normally available only in summer.)

At these prices, you'll want to be quite sure that you're ready to take the test! Your instructor is the best judge of this (see page 161).

Booking by phone

This method enables you to book a date there and then. (You'll receive written confirmation a few days later.) The person booking the test must be a credit card holder, and you'll need to give details of your provisional licence and Theory Test pass certificate, as well as any special needs or circumstances.

The number to ring is:
    0870 01 01 372.

The Extended Test

If you are convicted of dangerous driving, not only will you be disqualified from driving for a period, but when you are allowed to take your test again, it will be the **Extended Test**. This is longer than the standard test – about 70 minutes – and covers a wide variety of roads, usually including dual carriageways. The fee is also higher than for a standard test. Extra tuition from an ADI is recommended before attempting the Extended Test.

TEST YOUR UNDERSTANDING OF THIS SECTION

1. How long do you have after passing the Theory Test in which to take the Practical Test?

2. What is the pass mark for the Theory Test?

3. How can you best prepare for the Theory Test?

4. What is the procedure for booking a Practical Test?

5. Do you have any choice as to when you take your test?

Answers on page 202

What happens on 'the day'?

You'll be asked to sign a declaration that the insurance of your car is in order. Without this, the test can't proceed.

It's understandable that you might feel rather apprehensive when the day of your test comes round – after all, you've invested a lot of time and money in preparing for it, and passing it is an important step.

HOW TO PREPARE YOURSELF

Most people feel more confident if they're reasonably smartly dressed on the day of their driving test; and of course, it's important to wear comfortable shoes.

CHECKING OUT THE CAR

If you are taking your test in the driving school's car, your instructor will have made sure the requirements concerning the car have been complied with. These include:

- seat belts in good condition
- head restraints in correct position
- rear-view mirror in correct position
- additional rear-view mirror provided for examiner
- mechanically sound
- roadworthy, with MOT certificate if necessary (see 'Are you legal?', page 22)
- current tax disk displayed
- L-plates displayed (or D-plates optional in Wales)
- fully insured for you to drive.

THE PAPERWORK

You'll need to have with you:

- your provisional driving licence (*both* parts if you've got a photo licence)
- your Theory Test pass certificate
- additional photographic identity (ID), if your licence doesn't have a photo.

If you have to provide additional photographic ID, this can be a current signed passport, a railcard, credit card or other official signed card (e.g. student's union membership card). Or you can provide a photograph endorsed (signed and dated) by a person of official status such as a JP, local councillor, doctor, police officer, or minister of religion, with the words 'I _____ certify that this is a true likeness of _____, who has been known to me for __ months/years in my capacity as _____.'

But for most new drivers, this won't be necessary, as the DVLA now issue only photo licences. The complete licence, which you must produce when taking your test, consists of a photocard and a paper counterpart.

If you turn up for your test in an unsuitable vehicle, you will forfeit your test fee.

The last set exercise on the list is what used to be known as the three-point turn.

Don't worry about making a few mistakes. You can still pass your test as long as they are only minor driving faults.

SETTING STANDARDS

You may have wondered whether driving tests are completely fair.

The standards are monitored so that whatever examiner you get, or whatever test centre you go to, you should get the same result.

This explains why you might find a senior officer in the car as well as the examiner; he or she is not watching *you*, but checking that the examiner is doing his or her job properly.

THE TEST

A driving test lasts about **45 minutes**.

The first thing that happens is the **eyesight test** (see page 27).

After that, it's a case of driving along normal roads following the directions of the examiner; the roads are selected so as to provide a range of different conditions and a varied density of traffic, and suitable areas are chosen for you to carry out the set exercises.

Note: remember, it's your responsibility to *turn up on time* for your test. The seven slots are carefully timed throughout the day, to give time for the examiner to test you on all the necessary skills.

Set exercises

The examiner will tell you to pull up and stop, then he or she will explain the exercise to you before you do it:

● you *may or may not* be asked to perform an emergency stop
● you *will* be asked to perform two reversing exercises selected by the examiner from:
reversing round a corner;
reverse parking (behind a parked car, or into a marked bay);
turning in the road.

The rest of the test

Throughout the test, the examiner will be assessing:

● whether you are **competent** at controlling the car
● whether you are **making normal progress** for the roads you are on
● **how you react to any hazards** that occur in the course of the test
● whether you are **noticing** all traffic signs and signals, and **reacting** in the correct manner.

PERMISSION TO SPEAK?

Some people mistakenly believe that they're not allowed to talk to the examiner in the course of the test.

Clearly it wouldn't be right to chat at length, as this would affect your concentration; but you may need to ask the examiner to repeat something he or she has just said if you didn't hear clearly.

Obviously, it's much better to *ask* than to carry out the wrong manoeuvre.

The examiner may converse with you a little to try to put you at your ease, but this will probably be kept to a minimum; although *some* examiners are quite chatty – and if you find this distracting, just point it out politely. Like a job interview, a driving test is a somewhat strange and artificial situation, but provided you're fully prepared it shouldn't be too stressful.

BEING SURE YOU'RE READY TO TAKE THE TEST

This is where choosing a reliable qualified driving instructor is vital (see 'Choosing an instructor', page 29).

Completing a **log book** with your instructor and ticking off all the items on the test syllabus should help you feel confident that you're ready. (See 'Log book', page 24.)

You should feel:

- confident about driving in all conditions
- confident that you know your *Highway Code*
- confident that you can make decisions on your own about how to cope with hazards, without having to wait for your instructor to tell you what to do.

The requirements for passing your test are a combination of practical skills and mental understanding. The open road can be a risky environment, and your test result will show whether you're ready to go out there alone or whether you need a little more practice first.

TEST YOUR UNDERSTANDING OF THIS SECTION

1. What are the legal requirements concerning the car in which you take your driving test?

2. What documents must you take with you on the day of your test?

3. What does the first part of your driving test consist of?

4. Will you always have to perform an emergency stop as part of your test?

5. What are the reversing manoeuvres used in the test?

6. What will the examiner look for in your general driving?

7. Are you expected to drive without making any mistakes in order to pass?

8. When should you talk to the examiner in the course of your test?

9. How can a log book help you to know whether you are ready to take your test?

10. What should your attitude to driving be at the time of your test?

Answers on page 203–4

Passed/failed

PASSED?

Great news! You've just become a member of that 'Fellowship of the Road' we mentioned earlier; free to drive wherever you like, including on motorways; to tow a small trailer; and to drive vehicles weighing up to 3.5 tonnes.

Your reward is your **pass certificate**, and a copy of the **examiner's report** showing any minor faults you made during your test.

However exhilarated you feel about having passed, you'll find it useful to know where your minor weaknesses lie, so that you can concentrate on improving those aspects of your driving in the future.

ALONE AT LAST!

It can come as quite a shock to realise that you are now legally able to drive on your own, with no instructor or 'supervisor' beside you.

IN FACT – IT CAN BE QUITE SCARY!

Driving on a motorway for the first time can be a daunting experience (see 'Motorway rules', page 107).

In particular, the techniques for joining and leaving a motorway, lane use and overtaking are different from what you might have experienced up to now.

A good driving school will offer you the option of a post-test motorway lesson with your own instructor, and it makes sense to take advantage of this.

This motorway lesson, lasting two or three hours, represents the **minimum** of further training in driving; for more suggestions on how you could go on to improve the level of skill you've achieved so far, see the next section.

If you have booked a 'package' of driving lessons (see page 31), a free motorway lesson might form part of the deal. If you learn with the AA's Driving School, you will receive this benefit. Don't forget to make use of your free lesson!

FAILED?

Disappointing, certainly, but not the end of the world – many people don't pass their first test, but then sail through a second or third, having built on the experience of what it's like to take a test. You will probably feel more relaxed next time, helped by the knowledge that you've had more practice in those areas of driving where you weren't sufficiently skilled before.

Your driving instructor can listen to the examiner's explanation with you – it will help them direct the emphasis of the lessons leading up to your next test.

They're on *your* side – really!

The **driving test** has been improved to give a more realistic assessment of your driving ability, and to give you more chance to prove you can cope with all kinds of situations as a driver.

- The routes used have been extended to include sections of higher speed roads.
- The number of tests carried out in a day is now seven (previously eight), to give more time for each test.
- Examiners can choose to conduct all the set exercises in one place, so as not to use up time driving to another suitable location.

The **test report form** is designed to be as helpful and informative as possible.

It gives a printed record of all the skills assessed during the test, identifying any areas of weakness.

The examiner will also provide feedback in spoken form, and will explain to you what aspects of your driving are still in need of improvement.

HOW MANY MISTAKES GO TO MAKE UP A 'FAIL'?

In the case of a serious or dangerous fault –

just one!

In the case of less serious faults –

more than 15.

Less serious faults are known as 'driving faults' (previously they were called 'minor faults').

If you are faced with an unusually difficult or hazardous situation in the course of your test, that results in you making a driving fault, the examiner will take the circumstances into account when marking you for that part of the test.

Other faults can be 'dangerous' or 'serious'.

A **dangerous fault** is one that has caused actual danger to someone during the test.

A **serious fault** is one that didn't actually endanger anyone on this occasion, but could easily do so at another time. This can also cover 'habitual' driving faults – bad habits that show up in your driving that could cause a hazard.

So – it's clear that the way the driving test is organised is intended to ensure that people aren't out on the roads until they are safe drivers, who don't pose a danger to themselves or other road users.

If your test result shows that you're not quite at that stage, then don't lose heart. *Learn* from your mistakes, and get it right next time.

If you prepare thoroughly, with expert tuition from a qualified instructor and plenty of practice in between lessons, you'll maximise your chances of passing first time. But remember that the overall pass rate is less than 40%, so passing first time isn't the norm!

TEST YOUR UNDERSTANDING OF THIS SECTION

1. What will the examiner hand to you on completion of your test?

2. What can you do to make your first attempt at motorway driving less daunting?

3. What can you learn from verbal feedback given by the examiner after the test?

4. Why should you make sure you attend for your driving test on time?

5. What are 'driving faults', and how many are you allowed during your test?

Answers on page 205

Advanced driving skills – who needs them?

'Good driving is for life, not just for the test.'*

Driving is unusual among practical skills in that, once they've passed their test, most people *make no further attempt to improve their driving.*

Compare the way you approach any other hobby, or craft, or skill that you participate in regularly.

You'd expect to work at improving your skills so that in time you'd become an expert.

But in driving, people seem to assume that

> *everyone's an expert from the moment they pass their test!*

MOTIVATION

It's true that at present there is little to motivate people to improve their driving skills (but see Pass Plus, page 168).

'Research shows that about 35% of young drivers can be classed as unsafe, not because they don't know how to drive properly, but because they choose not to do so after they have passed their tests.'*

You might gradually start to make changes to the way you drive after a series of **near-misses** (see 'Motorists with attitude', page 50).

But it's possible to plan for improvement in a less risky, more methodical way, just as part of your day-to-day driving.

*Andrew Howard
AA Head of Road Safety Policy*

IMPROVING DRIVING STANDARDS FOR YOURSELF

Think of a routine journey that you carry out frequently.

Next time you're on that route, check the following points:

- Are you driving at the correct speed for the road?
- Are you keeping to the two-second rule?
- What are the places where you know you might meet a hazard?
- Are there any traffic signs you're not sure of?

Based on what you observe, make any necessary adjustments to your *road position* and *speed*.

Think about lane use and signalling at roundabouts and other junctions. Are your intentions always clear to other road users?

Start to *anticipate* regular hazards.

For example, if you know that a large concrete lorry usually pulls out of a particular junction every day, be prepared to slow down well in advance.

Make up some extra imaginary hazards and work out how you would respond to them.

If you've found any traffic signs you're not sure of, *look them up* in *The Highway Code,* or the DSA's book *Know Your Roadsigns.*

To sum up: try to *monitor your own standard of driving*, and see what you could do to improve it.

IMPROVING DRIVING STANDARDS THROUGH PASS PLUS

Pass Plus is a scheme set up in 1995 by the Driving Standards Agency and the Department of the Environment, Transport and the Regions. Planned in consultation with driving instructors and the insurance industry, it's aimed at encouraging people to go on training to **improve** their standard of driving during the first year after they pass their test.

At the time of writing, Pass Plus is divided into six sessions, each covering one module of the course.

Two modules deal with **attitude** and four with **skills**.

Attitude

The objective of these sessions is to highlight ways in which you can become a more *responsible* driver, and how you can show more *consideration* for other road users.

If you don't yet own your own car, but drive someone else's under their insurance, you can defer the Pass Plus concession and take it up later, as long as it's within two years.

Skills

The instructor builds on what you have already learned about *anticipation, observation* and *decision making,* progressing towards a more *positive approach* to driving.

Many insurers show their support for Pass Plus by offering a one-year no-claims **discount** on production of a pass certificate from the scheme.

You can get more information by calling 0115 901 2633.

ROSPA AND IAM

You could also consider taking an **advanced driving test** with the **Royal Society for the Prevention of Accidents (RoSPA)**, or the **Institute of Advanced Motorists (IAM)**.

You'll find details of groups in your area in the telephone directory.

If you don't want to take a test but would like an assessment of how you're doing after you've been driving for a while, then the **Guild of Experienced Motorists** is the organisation to contact. Or you might wish to contact the instructor who taught you to drive.

THRILLS WITHOUT SPILLS

If you'd like to try your hand at some fast driving in a safe environment, drop hints to friends and relatives that a day at the controls of a racing car would be a welcome birthday present – many circuits offer this experience.

You can also book some practice on a skid pan to find out how it feels when you have to control a skidding car (see 'On the skids', page 104). Your driving instructor or motoring organisations can point you in the right direction.

Any experience you can get of driving in new conditions or in different kinds of vehicles is valuable in building confidence, and will help to make you a better driver.

If you're driving some distance alone, always tell someone else where you're going and when you expect to arrive. This is a useful safety precaution.

Remember, a fine for speeding leads to penalty points on your licence. If you accumulate six penalty points within two years of passing your test, your licence will be revoked.

OUT IN THE COUNTRY

When you've passed your test you can start discovering some very different kinds of roads from the residential streets that most people become very familiar with while they're learning.

You'll have to negotiate **narrow lanes** in remote areas, where visibility is difficult and consideration for other drivers a must.

On **single-track roads**, passing places are indicated by a diamond-shaped sign. (See 'Giving way in normal driving', page 130.)

If there's a driver coming towards you, or you can tell that the driver behind is anxious to overtake:

- pull into a passing place on your left
- or wait just before a passing place on your right.

In addition:

- whenever possible, *give way* to vehicles coming *uphill*
- you may have to *reverse* back to a passing place to let an approaching vehicle pass.

And of course –

NEVER PARK IN A PASSING PLACE.

Be especially watchful for hazards on country roads, since some of the most remote places are also the most beautiful, and there may be large numbers of sightseers around.

Slow down for bends – they may be sharper than you think – and be on the look-out for **concealed junctions**.

Never let your speed build up on open roads to such an extent that you can't slow down in time when you arrive at a village, where a 30mph speed limit will apply.

GETTING AROUND

If you are heading off to an area you don't know well, plan the route in advance and take a good up-to-date road map with you. If you own a PC, you can print out a route from one of several route-planning programmes now available.

If you're travelling with a passenger, get him or her to navigate for you (but be aware that not everyone is a practised map-reader at first!).

And if you're on your own – try taping your route directions on a cassette to play in the car; this will avoid the necessity of taking your eyes off the road to look at the map while driving.

TEST YOUR UNDERSTANDING
OF THIS SECTION

1. Why do people view driving differently from the way they view other practical skills?

2. How can you improve your own standards of driving after you pass your test?

3. What is the Pass Plus scheme?

4. How should you use passing places on a single-track road?

5. What precautions should you take when setting out to drive for a long distance on your own?

Answers on page 206

Buying your first car

If you're happy to buy 'nearly-new', how about a low-mileage demonstration car?

This is going to represent a major financial commitment on your part, so of course you'll be keen to get it right.

Fortunately there's a wide range of resources you can draw on for advice, including:

- a local dealer or garage with a reputation for reliability
- general or specialist magazines, and features in newspapers
- television series that focus on comparisons of cars for value and reliability
- the internet.

So before you make your purchase –

do some research!

THE RIGHT CAR FOR YOU

You'll need to spend some time thinking about what kind of car you need.

- Would you prefer a manual or automatic gearbox? (See 'Can you handle it?', page 18.)
- Are you likely to want to tow a trailer? (See 'Shift that load!', page 137.)
- How many passengers do you need space for?
- Do you do most of your driving in town? If so, a small car that's economical on fuel is best.
- Or do you drive long distances in the country and on motorways? If so, a larger car might be more comfortable, and you might want to consider a deisel car, which may use up to 20% less fuel.

Other important considerations are:

- the **cost of insurance**
- the cost and availability of **spare parts**.

BUYING NEW

Brand-new cars can be very expensive, even compared with those just a few months old; the greatest depreciation in value takes place in the first few months.

However, you can shop around for good deals, especially just before it's time for a new registration letter to come in; and keen prices are available when you shop for cars on the internet.

If you can afford to buy new, you'll benefit from the latest improvements in safety and fuel consumption, and you'll have the safeguard of the warranty that comes with the car.

You should also shop around for finance packages if you're not paying cash. The AA can help you with this – even if you're not a member.

BUYING SECOND-HAND

The Australians call these 'pre-loved' cars, and obviously you'll hope your car *has* been looked after with loving care, not hammered and neglected!

There are several ways of going about the purchase of a second-hand car, including private sales, buying from dealers, and buying at auction.

If you are phoning up about a car you've seen advertised for sale, be aware that some dealers place advertisements pretending to be private sellers.

It's also possible
to buy a second-
hand car from
a new-car
dealer, if it's
been taken in
part-exchange.

Private sales

There is of course an element of risk in going down this route, but the main advantage is that prices will be lower.

Local free advertising papers can provide a useful overview of what's a fair price for a particular age and model of car, or you may be able to get hold of a specialist magazine.

Motoring organisations can help you here also: the **AA's Vehicle Inspection** service and **Used Car Data Check** can give you peace of mind before you buy. Qualified engineers will check out the car for safety and mechanical soundness, and provide a written report in around 24 hours.

The Used Car Data Check can tell you how many recorded keepers the vehicle has had, whether the colour has been changed, whether it's been recorded as a write-off for insurance, or if there is outstanding finance owing.

Buying from dealers

This may be more expensive, but you benefit from protection under the Sale and Supply of Goods Act (1994).

The dealer has to guarantee that:
- the car is of satisfactory quality and fit for its purpose
- any statements made about it are true and accurate.

The dealer may also offer a warranty on the car.

Auctions

Some very good deals can be picked up at car auctions, but it's a good idea to take someone with you who has experience of how they work.

Cars may be 'sold all good' or 'sold as seen'; 'sold all good' means you'll get a full service history and the car's true mileage will be shown. 'Sold as seen' usually applies to older cars with no warranty supplied.

Fleet cars

People tend to be wary of buying an ex-company car, and it's true that many will have been driven hard and have high mileages.

On the other hand, they will have been serviced regularly and may not have suffered from much short-journey driving. So a fleet car may be worth considering.

The internet

Large databases of used cars can be viewed on the net, and you can also get quotes for car finance and insurance packages.

SERVICING

Once you've bought your car, remember to keep up the services on a regular basis.

It's well worth building a good relationship with your local garage; they can get to know your car as well as you, and offer reliable advice when repairs need to be undertaken.

Remember to make all *regular checks* of the car yourself (see page 15 and pages 33–44).

If necessary, upgrade the *security precautions* – you don't want to lose your new car to a thief!

FINALLY –

Check you've completed all the necessary paperwork (see pages 22–6); and go on to enjoy a safe and happy motoring career!

TEST YOUR UNDERSTANDING
OF THIS SECTION

1. What considerations do you need to bear in mind when choosing your first car?

2. Why could it be a good idea to buy a car that runs on diesel?

3. When is the most expensive time to buy a new car?

4. What safeguards are available to you if you buy a used car from a dealer?

5. How can the internet be of use to you when buying a car?

Answers on page 207

Answers

Part 1

ANSWERS TO QUESTIONS ON 'GET INTO THE CAR...'

1. ABC stands for the order of the foot pedals from right to left: Accelerator, Brake, Clutch.
2. You should stop immediately if your oil warning light comes on. If you continue driving you will damage the engine.
3. You should check all the following regularly: the levels of oil and radiator coolant, the tyre pressures, the windscreen wipers and washers, all the front and rear lights (including number plate lights) and indicators, and the horn.
4. You check the oil by pulling out the dipstick and wiping it with a clean cloth; then return it to its place and pull out again, and look at the level showing between the markers. Don't forget: for an accurate reading, the car should be on a level road surface, and the engine cool.
5. The legally required tread depth is at least 1.6mm all round the tyre, and for three-quarters of the width across the centre of the tyre.

ANSWERS TO QUESTIONS ON 'CAN YOU HANDLE IT?'

1. Before you start the engine, check that the gear lever is in neutral and the handbrake on.

2. MSM stands for Mirror, Signal, Manoeuvre. This is the sequence you should follow before moving off, making a turn etc. Look in your rear view mirror – indicate, if necessary and if the way is clear – check over your shoulder (the blind spot) – and then move in the chosen direction.

3. There is almost always a blind spot somewhere in the driver's field of vision, so take a quick glance over your shoulder as well as checking the mirrors.

4. The driving test which came into effect in April 1999 asks you to carry out a reverse parallel parking manoeuvre, which could be the one in this question.

5. Start the car with the gear lever in 'Park' or 'Neutral', put your foot on the brake pedal, then select 'Drive' and smoothly release the brake. This may cause the car to start moving forward.

ANSWERS TO QUESTIONS ON 'ARE YOU LEGAL?'

1. Everyone preparing to learn to drive needs to apply for a provisional licence. You can get an application form from any Post Office.

2. Your driving instructor uses a log book to record your progress. The log book also contains a list of topics covered in the Theory Test.

3. The person who comes with you when you're practising in between lessons (your supervisor) doesn't need formal qualifications, but they must be over 21 and have held a full driving licence for at least three years.

4. An 'excess' on an insurance policy means that you have to pay a certain amount of the cost of repairs – say, the first £50 or £100 – in the event of an accident. Remember, with an insurance policy – read the small print!

5. The eyesight test will be done at the start of your driving test. You'll be asked to read a car number plate at a distance of 20.5 metres (about 67 feet). If you can't, your test will stop at that point.

ANSWERS TO QUESTIONS ON 'WHO'S IN CHARGE?'

1. You should look for an instructor who is fully qualified and a professional. You could try asking advice from friends who have recently learned to drive.

2. ADI stands for Approved Driving Instructor. Someone who displays the green certificate on their windscreen has passed the DSA's tests and so should be qualified to teach you to drive.

3. The car you learn to drive in must be insured for you to drive. You will be asked to sign a declaration about this before your driving test.

4. You aren't compelled by law to be taught by an ADI, but if money changes hands then your instructor must be an ADI, or at least a trainee (with a pink certificate).

5. The practical and theory tests have much in common, and learning what you need to know for one will reinforce your knowledge of the other. Your instructor can help by providing sample theory test questions for practice.

ANSWERS TO QUESTIONS ON 'LOOK AFTER YOUR CAR...'

1. The dipped beam headlights should be angled to the left (towards the kerb or verge) when you're driving in the UK, but if you travel to Europe and other countries where they drive on the right you'll need to fit converters on your headlights. Always remember to remove them as soon as you return to the UK.

2. Cars built since April 1980 should have one rear fog lamp fitted, although in practice many cars have two, and front ones as well. The rear fog lamp can be fitted centrally, or on the offside.

3. Since the coolant system is under pressure the temperature may sometimes reach nearly 100°C, but it should return to a lower level once you have been driving normally for a while. Always check the coolant level and if necessary top up the radiator (older cars) or the header tank of the cooling system (newer cars).

4. Power-assisted steering takes much of the hard work out of manoeuvring the car, and makes parking in tight spaces easier. Sometimes, however, if you lock the steering round too hard you may stall the car. Do not turn the steering wheel while the car is stationary.

5. In bad weather your windscreen rapidly becomes covered in spray from the vehicle in front, and you will not be able to see clearly to drive safely unless you can clear the screen at regular intervals. The problem is made worse when there is a low sun ahead.

6. In cars built after March 1987, rear seat belts must be fitted by law. Where there are rear seat belts available in the car, your passengers must wear them.

7. Catalytic converters are fitted in exhaust systems to make the emissions less harmful to the environment. Levels of carbon monoxide and hydrocarbons emitted are measured as part of the MOT test; the allowable levels are being tightened up further for newer cars.

8. When you arrive at the garage, you should switch off your engine and extinguish cigarettes. Do not use mobile phones.

9. You should stop filling the tank when the automatic cut-out operates. If you think the pump isn't working properly and your tank isn't full, seek advice from the garage staff.

10. You can demonstrate your commitment to helping the environment by having regular services and keeping the engine tuned, checking tyre pressures, driving without harsh acceleration or at excessive speeds, and by not carrying unnecessary weight such as an empty roof-rack. Plan your journeys to avoid congestion whenever possible, using route planners and heeding advice from organisations such as AA Roadwatch.

Part 2

ANSWERS TO QUESTIONS ON 'MOTORISTS WITH ATTITUDE'

1. Research has shown that young drivers tend to over-estimate their ability to anticipate and respond to hazards on the road. After about three years' experience it improves. Age is less important than experience. When drivers reach the age of 70 they have to re-apply for their licence, and do so again every three years.

2. There is no one 'right' speed – you should drive at or slightly below the speed limit for the road you are on. Be prepared to drive more slowly in built-up areas.

3. When driving on motorways it is easy to be intimidated by the high speed of other vehicles, and to think that you must drive faster than the speed limit in order to keep up.

4. 'Coasting' is unsafe because it reduces your control of the steering, which could lead to an accident.

5. 'Only a fool breaks the two-second rule' is a good line to memorise; it refers to keeping at least a two-second gap between your vehicle and the one in front and takes about two seconds to recite. However, you should double this gap in rain, and increase it ten times in icy conditions.

ANSWERS TO QUESTIONS ON
'I DIDN'T EVEN SEE HIM...'

1. Among the skills you need to be a safe driver are: anticipation, observation, concentration and forward planning. It may help if you memorise OAP – Observe, Anticipate, Plan.

2. Any of the following can cause you to stop concentrating fully on the road: the behaviour of pedestrians or passengers; roadside advertising; too much information to process all at once; and using mobile phones. In addition, if you've got something on your mind, you may start worrying about that problem and forget to give your full attention to your driving.

3. You should find a safe place to stop before making the call. It's not safe to carry on driving while using a mobile phone.

4. Six hours is too long to drive without a break; make a couple of rest stops on the way and you will feel better and improve your ability to concentrate. Don't just pull into a garage – get out at a safe place and walk around. And don't be tempted to speed up so as to get to the rest area more quickly – open the window to let in some fresh air.

5. In icy conditions, allow at least ten times the space you would usually allow between you and the car in front. Drive more slowly so that you won't skid if you have to brake. Use the technique of progressive braking. The road conditions can change unexpectedly and you may hit a patch of black ice. And, if you can avoid making the journey, don't drive in icy weather.

ANSWERS TO QUESTIONS ON 'IT'S IN THE RULES'

1. When two vehicles are approaching an unmarked junction from different directions, neither has priority. Use great caution as you cross, making use of 'right-left-right' observation.

2. You are allowed to enter a box junction before your exit is clear if you are turning right and you are only prevented (temporarily) by oncoming traffic.

3. You should wait until the car on the right has actually begun to turn; the driver might suddenly change his or her mind and go straight on, or they might have their left indicator on in error.

4. A long, narrow 'upside-down' triangle marked on the road warns you that there is a 'give way' junction just ahead.

5. If it will not impede the flow of following traffic, you can move into the correct lane by using 'Mirror, Signal, Manoeuvre'. But if you can see it's not safe to do so, you will have to stay in the wrong lane and find another route to your destination.

6. The key rule at roundabouts is 'Give way to traffic from the right'.

7. If the traffic sign marking a cycle lane has times of operation shown, you are allowed to use the lane outside those times.

8. Legally you are not required to stop if the pedestrian has not yet set foot on the crossing, but it is far better to get into the habit of slowing down and anticipating that a pedestrian may be waiting to cross, and then allowing them plenty of time to do so.

9. Nearly all road signs that give orders are circular. Red circles mean 'don't' and blue circles mean 'do'.

10. A broken white line is used to mark the centre of the road, and in a hazardous area the lines become longer between the gaps.

11. Street lights usually indicate a speed limit of 30mph.

12. The maximum national speed limit for single carriageway roads is 60mph; for dual carriageways and motorways, it's 70mph.

13. When towing a caravan, your speed limit is 10mph below the national speed limits for single carriageway roads and dual carriageways (50mph and 60mph respectively), although it is the same as for cars in built-up areas (30mph).

14. Although part of good driving skills is 'making normal progress', this does not mean that you should drive at the maximum allowed by the speed limit if the weather is bad; at night; on bends; or when driving a large vehicle. You should always adjust your speed to the conditions.

15. A car can legally tow as much as its own weight. However, you should check the manufacturer's recommendations for your vehicle, and remember that some towed items (especially caravans) are more unstable than others, so it is better to tow less weight than the maximum allowed. Towing will affect the way your vehicle handles. You may need to take another test in order to tow over a certain weight; check the towing limitations shown on your licence.

ANSWERS TO QUESTIONS ON 'YOU CAN'T PARK THERE!'

1. Park as close to the kerb as possible, with your wheels parallel to it. Avoid parking with your wheels half-on and half-off the kerb.

2. In town centres, make use of car parks, meter zones and 'park-and-ride' schemes. In towns, rectangular signs with a white letter 'P' on a blue background guide you to the car parks.

3. You may not park in a 'Disabled' space (one reserved for a driver who displays a Blue Card) at any time. Nor are you allowed to do so if you remain with your car.

4. If you are parked in the street at night in an area where the speed limit is 30mph, and you have parked correctly facing in the same direction as the flow of traffic, then you do not need to leave sidelights on.
    Note: you must be parked at least 10 metres (32 feet) away from any junction. If your vehicle is towing a trailer, you must have your sidelights on. You must do so also if the speed limit in the area is greater than 30mph.

5. If you have to park on a hill, leave the car in gear to prevent it rolling away. Use a forward gear if facing up hill; if facing down hill, put the car in reverse. Turn the wheels towards the kerb if facing up hill.

ANSWERS TO QUESTIONS ON 'DRIVING UNDER THE INFLUENCE'

1. The UK police don't currently have the power to carry out breath tests completely at random – although this is done in some other countries. But they may ask you to take a test if they have reasonable cause to suspect you have been drinking and driving, or intend to do so. Breath tests are always carried out at the scenes of accidents.

2. 'How to avoid being caught' is an example of asking the wrong sort of question. Ensure that the evening is both safe and enjoyable for all concerned by agreeing on someone who won't drink alcohol that evening to be the driver. Or, you could use public transport or taxis.

3. If you drink alcohol in the evening it's quite possible that you will still be over the limit the following morning; this will almost certainly be the case if you drink heavily.

4. Your coordination, reaction speed and hazard awareness will all be affected, as well as your ability to judge distance and speed. You may well feel over-confident about your skill as a driver and take more risks than normal, posing a danger to yourself, to other drivers and pedestrians. Remember: drinking and night driving often go together, and it's more difficult to spot hazards in the dark.

5. Although you are safer taking medicine prescribed for you rather than for someone else, you should still check the label and/or ask your doctor's advice about driving.

ANSWERS TO QUESTIONS ON 'IT'S DIFFERENT AT NIGHT'

1. You should take even more care when driving at night because hazards are more difficult to see in the dark; pedestrians are more difficult to *see*, and may be less predictable in their behaviour.

2. Dipped headlights are used at all times at night except: on restricted roads with a speed limit of 30mph or less and where street lamps are not more than 185 metres (600 feet) apart; on roads with no street lights when you could dazzle vehicles ahead; and in the daytime in dull or rainy conditions.

3. Generally you would not expect to use full beam headlights on a motorway, as even on unlit sections you will almost always be driving in a stream of traffic.

4. Fog lights should only be used in fog or poor visibility; you should switch them off again as soon as you can see clearly. 'Poor visibility' as defined by *The Highway Code* is when you cannot see further ahead than 100 metres (328 feet).

5. Your knowledge of the traffic ahead can sometimes be improved at night because you can see oncoming vehicles by their headlights – sometimes before they have rounded a corner ahead of you. However, your peripheral vision is reduced to what you can see from the beams of your own headlights.

ANSWERS TO QUESTIONS ON 'STORMY WEATHER'

1. You should double the time you allow for braking and stopping when driving on a wet road. For driving on ice, allow as much as ten times the normal stopping distance.

2. If you find your car has gone into a skid, ease off the brake or accelerator and steer smoothly in the same direction as the skid. If your car has anti-lock brakes it may be possible to continue braking firmly while you steer out of the skid.

3. First decide whether your journey is really necessary; if it is, clear all snow and ice from the vehicle and demist the windscreen thoroughly before you start out. Carry food, drink, warm clothes and boots or stout shoes in case of emergencies, as well as a spade for digging the car out of drifts.

4. In fog drivers can quickly become disorientated, and may start to follow closely behind the rear lights of the car in front as it makes them feel more secure. This can be dangerous, as you need to have enough space to stop suddenly. If you have to slow down yourself, use your mirror first and brake slowly if possible, as other cars may be following too closely behind you for the reason given above.

5. As soon as you have driven out of fog, switch off your rear fog lights, as they are too bright for normal use and will dazzle other drivers. The use of rear fog lights can have the effect of preventing your brake lights being visible.

ANSWERS TO QUESTIONS ON 'MOTORWAY RULES'

1. Learner drivers are not allowed on motorways; along with motor cycles under 50cc, tractors, horse riders, cyclists and pedestrians. But learners can observe how motorway driving is different from other driving when they are passengers in someone else's car; and immediately after passing the test it's a good idea to have at least one motorway lesson with your instructor. Driving on some dual carriageways can provide a similar experience.

2. Before starting a long motorway journey carry out all the standard checks on your car; driving at high speed for long distances can increase the risk of breakdowns, and motorway tailbacks can make engine overheating more likely.

3. You should join the motorway by building up your speed to fit in with the flow of traffic in the left lane; indicating right; and then moving across when there is a space or someone moves to the centre lane to let you in. Give way to traffic already on the motorway rather than speeding up to cut in. Once you have joined, stay in the left lane so that you can adjust to the higher driving speed. Show the same courtesy to other drivers joining the motorway.

4. It would be very dangerous to stop and retrieve a suitcase that has fallen from your roof rack on to the motorway. Stop at the next telephone and contact the police (*The Highway Code* tells you to use the direct phones provided and not your mobile phone).

5. There are no times when you should overtake on the left, but you are allowed to keep up with traffic in a lane which happens to be moving faster than the lane to the right for a period of time. This may happen when all traffic in the left lane is leaving the motorway at the next exit, but both lanes to the right are filled with slow-moving traffic.

6. A red cross over a lane means that you cannot drive in that lane. Green or white arrows indicate lanes which are available to traffic.

7. After leaving the motorway to the left, you will usually come to a roundabout or other road system with a green sign telling you which way to turn to continue your journey.

8. Plenty of warning is given when a motorway lane is closed ahead. Move into the lane(s) indicated in good time; much frustration can be caused by drivers leaving it to the last possible minute to change lanes, resulting in hold-ups.

9. On a motorway, green reflective studs mark sliproads. They are used elsewhere to mark side roads and lay-bys. At night or in poor visibility, looking at the colour of the reflective studs can help you to work out where you are on the road.

10. You may not stop on the hard shoulder unless you have broken down; it should not be used by anyone who feels like a cigarette, to swap drivers or because children say they can't wait till the service area. Stop as far to the left as possible, switch on your hazard warning lights, and get everyone out of the vehicle and well away from the motorway (animals should be left in the vehicle). Contact the police via the emergency phone; the markers indicate the direction of the nearest one. If you are unable to get your vehicle off the carriageway and on to the hard shoulder, switch on hazard warning lights and leave the vehicle only when safe. Do not put a warning triangle on the motorway.

Part 3

ANSWERS TO QUESTIONS ON 'HOW AM I DRIVING?'

1. Drivers arriving from countries where they drive on the right are at risk of being disorientated when they drive off the ferry, or drive away from the airport. Keep at a safe distance and don't sound your horn or flash your lights at the driver, as he or she may be tired from travel and struggling to cope with unfamiliar road signs.

2. Arm signals are used infrequently by car drivers but are used all the time by horse riders, cyclists etc. As a car driver you need to be completely familiar with the signals used by these other road users. Use arm signals when necessary to reinforce indicator signals. A full list of arm signals is given in *The Highway Code*, including those for letting anyone controlling traffic know your intentions.

3. The police will direct you to pull over by using flashing blue lights and left indicators. Check that it is safe to pull over, then stop and switch off your engine. Remember to have the legally required documents to hand; any that you are not carrying with you may be produced at a police station within seven days.

4. A 'rat-run' is a minor road, usually in a residential area, which drivers use in an attempt to get ahead in queuing traffic. This results in further blockages as the cars rejoining the major road from the 'rat run' attempt to 'push in', causing additional frustration at busy times. The risk to pedestrians, especially school children, from speeding cars, is also increased. Traffic-calming measures such as speed humps are being introduced to deter drivers from using 'rat-runs'.

5. You should always anticipate bends, and any other potential hazard, by slowing down in a controlled manner so that you can steer round the bend at a safe speed. Brake as you approach the bend, then start to apply the accelerator gently while in the bend. If you are driving too fast round the bend you are likely to cross the centre line and cause a hazard to oncoming drivers.

ANSWERS TO QUESTIONS ON 'I'M RIGHT BEHIND YOU!'

1. Tailgating means driving too close behind another vehicle, often with an intent to intimidate or harass the driver. It is dangerous because if you are too close you will not have enough room to stop in an emergency, especially if the road is wet or icy. If you get too close behind a large vehicle you will not be able to see the road ahead well enough to overtake it safely.

2. Flashing your headlights could intimidate the other driver and cause them to lose concentration, thus making accidents more likely to happen. Using full beam headlights when driving behind another car will produce a dazzling glare in their rear view mirror which is dangerous. The technique of driving very close and flashing headlights is often used by impatient drivers on a motorway when they wish to dislodge someone they consider too slow from the centre or right lane; at motorway speeds, this is also a dangerous practice.

3. Hazard warning lights are intended for use when the car is stationary and causing an obstruction. They should not be used while driving, except for short periods on a motorway or unrestricted dual carriageway, to warn other drivers of a hazard ahead.

4. You should sound your horn only in emergencies, or to let other road users know you are there.

5. Normally you should never sound the horn when your car is stationary, but you are allowed to do so in order to prevent an accident if you see a vehicle approaching which is likely to put you in danger.

ANSWERS TO QUESTIONS ON 'IT'S NOT ME, IT'S THE OTHERS!'

1. Flashing your headlights in annoyance at someone who has overtaken you and then cut in ahead of you is a criminal offence, because it goes against one of the rules in *The Highway Code* where the words 'MUST NOT' are printed in red (followed by a reference to the relevant law). So, although the other driver has also acted against *The Highway Code*, it's advisable to practice 'defensive driving' and keep on the right side of the law yourself.

2. Although a truck driver may use flashing left indicators as a signal that it is safe for you to overtake, you should only do so when you can see clearly that the road ahead is clear and that there is plenty of room to complete the manoeuvre. Drivers of slow vehicles should pull over and stop to let traffic pass when they find a safe place to do so.

3. In wet weather you should double the 'two-second rule' about how long it takes to stop, and in icy conditions you need to multiply the time of two seconds by ten.

4. You should allow at least as much room when overtaking a motorcyclist – a car's width – as you would for a car, because the motorcyclist may swerve, or be blown towards you by high winds.

5. Once you are sure it is safe to overtake, you should proceed confidently, get past the other vehicle and return to your normal position without 'cutting in'. If you begin an overtaking manoeuvre and then hesitate or lose your nerve, you could be a hazard to other drivers.

ANSWERS TO QUESTIONS ON 'WHO GOES FIRST?'

1. That the pedestrian is elderly is not the most important factor here. If the pedestrian is waiting on the pavement, you can continue round the corner if it would be unsafe to do otherwise because of following traffic; but if you can safely slow down and let the pedestrian cross first, then do so. If, on the other hand, the pedestrian is already crossing the side road, then he or she has priority. But remember: don't wave anyone across.

2. Always give way to trams – they cannot steer to avoid you. Do not attempt to overtake them, especially on the inside if they have stopped to pick up passengers at a tram stop in the centre of the road. Get to know the signs that are meant just for tram drivers.

3. Give way to cyclists in cycle lanes and on toucan crossings. Stay well back from a cyclist who has indicated that he or she wishes to change lanes, or when you are approaching a junction or roundabout behind a cyclist.

4. Horse riders are permitted to ride two abreast, though they must drop back to single file on narrow roads or when approaching a bend. The outer of the two riders may be shielding a younger or less experienced person.

5. You should stop and switch off your engine when asked to do so by someone in charge of farm animals. (After all, there is little point in doing anything else!)

6. A long vehicle will pull out to the right in preparation for turning left (although it would be incorrect to do so in a car). Slow down and give way to the long vehicle.

7. You should wait until your view of the major road is completely clear before pulling out. Your view will be obscured until the vehicle has finished turning into the side road.

8. Use your mirrors to anticipate the ambulance's path through the traffic, then pull over and slow down or pause if it is safe to do so.

9. Double mini-roundabouts should be treated as two separate roundabouts. At each one, give way to traffic from the right.

10. The sign indicating 'Priority over oncoming traffic' is a blue rectangle with a large white 'up' arrow on the left next to a smaller red 'down' arrow.

ANSWERS TO QUESTIONS ON 'ROAD USERS AT RISK'

1. Cyclists and motorcyclists are more vulnerable than car drivers because they have little protection, they can be blown off course by strong winds, and they are often riding outside the car driver's field of vision. An object as thin as a lamp-post can obscure your view of a cyclist or motorcyclist.

2. Be on the look-out for children in residential areas, on their way to or from school, or playing in the street. Be aware that they do not always realise the danger from cars, and may run out into the street unexpectedly.

3. A red triangular sign with silhouette figures of two children running is used to warn of a school crossing patrol ahead. (The word 'Patrol' appears on a plate beneath the sign on the approach to a school.)

4. It is thought that the improved safety features of today's cars, aimed at reducing the risk of serious injury from impacts, can lead to a false sense of security in young drivers, making them more likely to drive dangerously.

5. A pedestrian hit by a car travelling at 40mph is likely to be killed. Every mph by which you reduce your speed in built-up areas reduces the likelihood of your inflicting serious injury on another person in the event of an accident.

ANSWERS TO QUESTIONS ON 'SHIFT THAT LOAD!'

1. When towing a caravan or trailer you have to allow for the effect of the extra length and weight when you are manoeuvring, turning or parking. All will require even more care and concentration than usual, as well as an awareness of other road users.

2. 'Snaking' is the word used to describe what happens when a caravan being towed at too high a speed begins to swerve out of control. This may also happen as a result of high winds. The driver must ease off the accelerator and brake gently while regaining control of the steering. Always observe the appropriate speed limit, which is 10mph lower than for cars not towing trailers (on any road with a speed limit higher than 30mph).

3. The weight should be distributed as evenly as possible, to minimise the risk of losing control. The load should be safely secured and should not stick out in a dangerous manner.

4. Passengers are not allowed to ride in a trailer while it is on tow, so you cannot use your caravan as additional seating for people travelling with you. All passengers must ride inside the car and wear seat belts.

5. When parking with a trailer, take care not to inconvenience others. The trailer must have lights on overnight.

ANSWERS TO QUESTIONS ON 'IT'S YOUR RESPONSIBILITY'

1. When you have a child passenger who is under 14, you are responsible for their safety, even if their parent is a passenger as well. It's up to you to make sure they are properly secured by a seat belt or by the appropriate child restraint.

2. Appropriate restraints include child seats, harnesses and baby seats of approved design. For very small children a booster seat suitable for their weight can be positioned on the back seat.

3. It is better to use an adult seat belt in the rear of the car than no restraint at all; but try to avoid carrying children in any way that could place them at risk of injury.

4. It is not safe to carry children behind the rear seat of a hatchback, as they cannot be strapped in, and could be thrown forward in the event of an accident or emergency stop.

5. A rear-facing baby seat should never be positioned in a front seat that has an air-bag installed, since the air-bag, if inflated, could cause the child to suffocate.

ANSWERS TO QUESTIONS ON 'TRUST ME, I'M A FIRST-AIDER'

1. Bandages, plasters, safety-pins, scissors, sterile dressings, antiseptic wipes, disposable gloves. A ready-assembled first aid kit should contain these items.

2. There is a high risk of fire at an accident scene, and any spilt fuel could be ignited by a spark from a cigarette.

3. When calling the emergency services, be ready to give the location of the accident as fully as you can, and say how many vehicles are involved and how many people are injured.

4. You should not move casualties unless you know there is an immediate danger of fire or explosion.

5. ABC stands for Airway, Breathing, Circulation. This is a good way to remember the First Aid procedure.

6. Do not give an accident victim anything to eat or drink.

7. Warning triangles should be positioned with great care, at least 45 metres behind your car on the same side of the road. They should not be used on motorways. In some countries it's a legal requirement to carry a warning triangle in your car.

8. You should provide your name and address, and that of the vehicle's owner if different, to anyone at an accident scene with reasonable grounds for requesting them.

9. If police do not attend at the accident scene you have 24 hours in which to report the accident to them; but you should not wait that long unless you have any good reason, but rather report it as quickly as possible.

10. The hard shoulder is a highly dangerous place for pedestrians, and you would cause a hazard by attempting to change a wheel there. You should request assistance using the emergency phone, then wait in a safe place well back from the motorway. Breakdown assistance can be expensive if you are not a member of a motoring organisation.

Part 4

ANSWERS TO QUESTIONS ON 'APPLYING FOR YOUR TEST'

1. When you have passed your Theory Test, you have two years in which to take and pass your Practical Test. If you did not do so within that time, you would have to start again by taking another Theory test.

2. The pass mark for the Theory Test can change from time to time, so it's best to ask your instructor when you sit the test. But usually you have to get about 85% of the answers right – currently 30 of the 35 questions.

3. The Theory Test is conducted using a touch-screen to answer 35 multiple-choice questions in 40 minutes. The questions cover all aspects of driving and knowledge about road safety, and answering them correctly demands a thorough knowledge of *The Highway Code*.

4. You can book your Practical Test using an application form provided by your ADI; forms are also available from any DSA driving test centre. Alternatively, you can book by credit card over the phone; your appointment will be confirmed by letter shortly afterwards.

5. Whichever method you use to book, you can state what day and time would be most convenient for your test, and which dates are not possible for you. The cost is higher if you want to take your test in the evening or on a Saturday. Note that not all test centres offer these options.

ANSWERS TO QUESTIONS ON 'WHAT HAPPENS ON 'THE DAY'?'

1. The car you take your test in must be mechanically sound and roadworthy, and display an up-to-date tax disc and L-plates. It must be fully insured for you to drive. A rear-view mirror and head restraints must be provided for the examiner's use.

2. You must take with you your licence and Theory Test pass certificate. If you have a licence with a photo included, take both the card and the paper counterpart. If not, you will require additional photographic proof of identity.

3. The first part of your driving test is an eyesight test; if you do not pass this, the test cannot proceed further. The examiner will ask you to read a car number plate at a distance of 20.5 metres.

4. An emergency stop will not necessarily be one of your set exercises – about one out of three candidates will be asked to perform this.

5. You will have to perform two out of three of the reversing manoeuvres: reversing round a corner, reverse parking behind a parked car or into a marked bay, and turning in a road.

6. The examiner will assess how well you control the car, react to hazards, and respond to signals and instructions. He or she will expect you to drive at an appropriate speed for the road you are on – not too fast, but not too slow, as this would impede other traffic and indicate that you are not yet ready for independent driving.

7. It is expected that you will make a few minor mistakes during your test. Any major or dangerous mistakes would cause you to fail the test.

8. If you do not hear something that the examiner asks you to do, don't be afraid to ask them to repeat it. However, don't talk more than necessary as this would affect your concentration.

9. The log book provides a systematic record for you and your instructor of the aspects of driving that you have mastered. When you can tick off everything, you are ready to take the test.

10. By the time you take your test you should feel confident about your ability to control the car in all situations, and about driving independently; you must be able to make decisions without needing to wait for instructions.

ANSWERS TO QUESTIONS ON 'PASSED/FAILED'

1. The examiner will give you your pass certificate, if you have been successful in the test, and a report with a printed explanation of your performance. The report is given to all candidates.

2. You can make your first drive on the motorway less daunting by booking a motorway lesson with your regular instructor. For the first time you drive on the motorway after that, try to find a time when the motorway is relatively quiet, so that you can join without too much difficulty, and perhaps leave at the next exit. Do not attempt long hours of motorway driving immediately after passing your test; build up experience gradually.

3. The examiner will talk through the good and bad points of your driving during the test; this will help you focus on aspects to improve, whether or not you have passed. If your instructor is there to listen with you, this adds to the value of the information received.

4. The seven driving test 'slots' are carefully timed throughout the day, so that all the exercises and other requirements can be fitted into the 47 minutes. This is why it is important to be on time.

5. 'Driving faults', previously called 'minor faults', are those mistakes you make during your test which are not considered serious enough for you to fail. However, if you commit more than 15, you will not pass the test.

ANSWERS TO QUESTIONS ON 'ADVANCED DRIVING SKILLS – WHO NEEDS THEM?'

1. In most sports or hobbies people expect to upgrade their skills regularly, but in driving the common perception is that once you have passed your test, that's all you need to learn. This is in part because learning to drive costs a great deal of money, and people are unwilling to expend any more on further training.

2. You should try to look objectively at the way you drive and consider how you could improve your skills of observation, anticipation and consideration for other road users. Check whether there are any road signs on your route that you are unsure of, and check your speedometer to see that you are observing speed limits.

3. Pass Plus is a government-sponsored scheme administered by the DSA which aims to improve driving skills by a course of a minimum of six lessons with an instructor, taken in the first year after passing your test. The scheme has the backing of many insurers, who offer a variety of discounts to drivers presenting a pass certificate showing they have completed Pass Plus.

4. When driving on single-track roads, consideration and cooperation are vital. Pull into passing places where possible to let others proceed, or wait just ahead of one on the opposite side if more appropriate. Always give way to traffic coming uphill if possible. Never use the passing places to park and admire the view – look out for areas marked 'Viewpoint'.

5. When driving for a long distance alone, plan your route in advance and write down directions or record them on a cassette. Tell someone else where you are going and when you expect to arrive, or print out a route and leave a copy with them. A mobile phone is useful for calling your motoring organisation in the event of a breakdown, but make sure you give your precise location when you call. Remember to carry emergency supplies, including water. Do not drive for too long without a break.

ANSWERS TO QUESTIONS ON 'BUYING YOUR FIRST CAR'

1. Consider what type of car you need for the sort of driving you do; how many passengers, whether you drive short or long distances, and whether you need to tow a trailer. Decide whether you would prefer a manual or automatic gearbox. High-speed performance cars are inappropriate for town driving, and lead to excessive speed and accidents.

2. Diesel cars are best for long-distance runs; they are more economical in terms of fuel consumption than petrol cars. However, the initial cost of the vehicle is likely to be higher.

3. New cars are most expensive at the time when new registrations come in – currently 1 March and 1 September.

4. Second-hand cars bought from dealers are covered by the Sale and Supply of Goods Act, 1994. They must be of satisfactory quality, fit for their purpose and any statements concerning the car must be true and accurate.

5. A warranty may be provided by the dealer. It is often cheaper to buy new cars on the internet, and you can make your choice at your leisure without feeling under pressure from salespeople. Finance packages and car insurance can also be purchased in this way. Large databases of second-hand cars are available on the net.

Index